FLORIDA STATE
UNIVERSITY LIBRARIES

DEC 28 1998

TALLAHASSEE, FLORIDA

*In Praise
of Difference*

In Praise of Difference

The Emergence of a Global Feminism

ROSISKA DARCY DE OLIVEIRA

Translated by Peggy Sharpe

Rutgers University Press
New Brunswick, New Jersey, and London

First published in Portuguese in 1991 as *Elogio da diferença—O feminino emergente* by Editora Brasiliense, São Paulo, Brazil
First published in English in 1998 by Rutgers University Press, New Brunswick, New Jersey

Library of Congress Cataloging-in-Publication Data

Oliveira, Rosiska Darcy de.
 [Elogio de diferença. English]
 In praise of difference : the emergence of a global feminism / Rosiska Darcy de Oliveira ; translated by Peggy Sharpe.
  p. cm.
 Includes bibliographical references.
 ISBN 0-8135-2557-8 (alk. paper).—ISBN 0-8135-2558-6 (pbk. : alk. paper)
 1. Feminism. 2. Femininity. I. Sharpe, Peggy. II. Title.
 HQ1154.0395713 1999
 305.42—DC21   98-15616
                                                              CIP

British Cataloging-in-Publication information available from the British Library.

Copyright © 1998 by Rosiska Darcy de Oliveira
This translation copyright © 1998 by Rutgers, The State University
All rights reserved
No part of this book may be reproduced or utilized in any form or by any means, electronic or mechanical, or by any information storage and retrieval system, without written permission from the publisher. Please contact Rutgers University Press, Livingston Campus, 100 Joyce Kilmer Avenue, Piscataway, New Jersey 08854-8099. The only exception to this prohibition is "fair use" as defined by U.S. copyright law.
Manufactured in the United States of America

For Miguel, this book which we wove together with the thick thread of our life.

CONTENTS

Translator's Preface   ix

1 Introduction   1
2 Sexual Dichotomy and Inequality   9
3 The Equality Trap   39
4 The Emergence of the Feminine   79
5 Antigone and the Androgyne   127

Notes   133
Bibliography   137

TRANSLATOR'S PREFACE

Like Antigone in Sophocles' play of the same name, and whose name appears throughout the pages of the following essay, Rosiska Darcy de Oliveira experienced first-hand the consequences of transgressing against the law when she was exiled by the Brazilian military dictatorship in 1969, two years after completing her law degree at the Pontífica Universidade Católica of Rio de Janeiro. Darcy de Oliveira's exile exemplifies the destiny of an entire generation of vibrant, young intellectuals whose academic and professional lives were temporarily, and in many cases permanently disrupted during the years of dictatorship following the 1964 military coup in Brazil. Accused of leaking information to the international press about torture and censorship under the newly established military regime, thereby contributing to the denigration of Brazil's image overseas, Rosiska and her husband, the sociologist Miguel Darcy de Oliveira, spent the next fourteen years in exile in Geneva, Switzerland.

According to Darcy de Oliveira's testimony, the anguish and loneliness of the experience of exile was attenuated by her active involvement in the European feminist movement which brought together women from many different cultures.[1] Indeed, it appears that she profited as much from the affective bonds she formed with other women during these years as she did from the academic and professional opportunities that became available to her in Geneva. In 1974, she pursued graduate studies at the Institut d'Études du Développement of the University de Geneva; and in 1987 she completed her Ph.D. at the Faculté de Psychologie et Sciences de l'Education. She organized the first course in women's studies at the University of Geneva and, from 1973 to 1983, she taught and carried out research in women's studies. During this time, she also maintained an active international lecture schedule, speaking out against the Brazilian military dictatorship on every continent of the world. In short, Darcy de Oliveira transformed her exile into fertile terrain for continued transgression.

In 1983, four years after the declaration of amnesty by the new civilian government, Darcy de Oliveira returned to her native city of Rio de Janeiro where she again took up her life as a teacher, activist, writer, and intellectual, ascending to even greater national and international prominence. Darcy de Oliveira's academic and professional credentials speak for themselves most eloquently. She has published in Portuguese, English, and French; two of her books appeared in Europe after her return to Brazil: *Le féminin ambigu* (1989) and *La culture des femmes* (1992). Today Darcy de Oliveira is professor of literature at the Pontífica Universidade Católica of Rio de Janeiro. A member of the Council on Women's Rights of the State of Rio de Janeiro since 1991, she is also a well-known advocate of women's rights. In 1995, when Fernando Henrique Cardoso, a fellow former European sojourner, became president of Brazil, Darcy de Oliveira was named president of the Conselho Nacional dos Direitos da Mulher (National Council on Women's Rights), a federally sponsored initiative with headquarters at the Ministry of Justice in Brasília.

Twelve years, both in Europe and in Brazil, as director of

the nongovernmental organization IDAC, Instituto de Ação Cultural (Institute of Cultural Action), had given Darcy de Oliveira the experience necessary for her work as president of the National Council on Women's Rights. IDAC, known generically as an ONG (a nongovernmental organization), cofounded by Darcy de Oliveira and Paulo Freire, addressed issues of cultural importance to the Brazilian people which were not being sufficiently supported by government, business, or international funding agencies. Transferred to Brazil after the declaration of amnesty in 1979, IDAC is similar to other ONGs that have developed throughout Latin America over the past two decades. According to Miguel Darcy de Oliveira, these nongovernmental organizations represent an attempt to construct "a new world civil society which is capable of asserting itself as a social actor vis-à-vis government and business. The ONGs thereby contribute to the democratization of an unjust, exclusionary, international order which is submissive to the game of power and the laws of the market place."[2]

Among the many initiatives Darcy de Oliveira coordinated as director of IDAC was a cultural program for women called "Projeto Mulher" ("Project Woman"). This was the foundation of "Planeta Fêmea" ("Female Planet"), a forum that became an international task force on Women, Democracy, Environment, and Development and played an active role at the "United Nations Conference on the Environment" held in Rio de Janeiro in 1992, as well as at the "International Conference on Women: Equality, Development, and Peace" held in China in 1995. In China, Darcy de Oliveira and Ruth Cardoso, wife of President Cardoso, presided over the Brazilian delegation. Darcy de Oliveira also served as a member of the Brazilian delegation to the "United Nations Conference on Population and Development" in Cairo in 1994, and to the "Conference on Social Development" in Copenhagen in 1995. Currently, she consults on issues related to women and development for various international agencies such as the Inter-American Development Bank, the World Health Organization, and UNESCO.

Since the 1970s, Darcy de Oliveira has lectured in many countries on topics such as cultural action and community development, women and the ecological movement, and women and literature. Her contributions to projects related to women and development have also been recognized within Brazil where she has been the recipient of several prestigious honors and awards, including the Order of Rio Branco from the Brazilian Ministry of Foreign Relations, the Nísia Floresta Medal from the Government of the State of Rio Grande do Norte, and the Tiradentes Medal from the Legislative Assembly of the State of Rio de Janeiro.

In Praise of Difference: The Emergence of a Global Feminism originally appeared in Portuguese in 1991. Darcy de Oliveira traces the marginalization of the feminine universe back to the classical figure of Antigone, whose transgression into forbidden territory—the public sphere—was punished by death. Antigone's vision of justice serves as the landscape upon which the author formulates the concept of the feminine as a paradigm for social change in contemporary society. Writing at the end of the twentieth century, Darcy de Oliveira sees Western women entangled in a search for identity that has resulted, paradoxically perhaps, in extensive reassessment of the traditional values of the feminine that have been used to demarcate women's boundaries and restrict their access to the public sphere throughout Western civilization. Although she refutes the binary, prescriptive logic of the established parameters of the masculine and the feminine, Darcy de Oliveira comes out in favor of women's search for their identity through, or as a result of, their difference.

Upon examining the major sociological and historical advances championed by the women's movement in Europe and North America during the nineteenth and twentieth centuries, the author observes that women's attempts to restructure their personal and professional lives to accord with the values prescribed by traditional masculine culture have led them straight into, what she calls, an equality trap. With the help of interdisciplinary research from sociology, psychology, linguistics, and literary theory, Darcy de Oliveira reveals the mixed messages embedded in the concept of gender equality that has constituted women's model for change in the second half of the twentieth century and which, according to Darcy de Oliveira, has led women to the brink of a collective psychosocial identity crisis. To meet this crisis, she calls for a revalorization of the ancestral feminine, of the values and ethics of the private sphere which have been dismissed as inferior, outdated, and inappropriate in the public sphere.

Balance and harmony in society will improve insofar as women move toward an identity, that is yet to be constructed, but is grounded in a concept of equality built not on likeness, or on imitation, but on difference without hierarchy—a "feminism of difference." Hence the title *In Praise of Difference*. This more dynamic phase of the women's movement will "feminize the world" as it makes possible the kind of social and cultural transformations that women's earlier struggles for equality could never have achieved.

Darcy de Oliveira critiques the concept of androgyny as a model for women's identity-formation and challenges society to rethink the psychoanalytical postulations of French feminists for whom the body and the psychic qualities of the feminine are as important as the social roles women have played for centuries. Moreover, she warns against placing a market value on nurturing and caretaking, fearing that further commercialization of these values will destabilize and devaluate them, thereby threatening the very existence of the private realm with its emphasis on interpersonal relationships, intimacy, and the affective nature of human relations. Her "project of difference" presupposes a newly constructed identity born of interaction with others. Furthermore, she believes that rethinking the values of the traditional feminine role of nurturer/caretaker does not imply that women are losing ground; rather that they are involved in a process of reconsidering what is truly valuable about the ways in which they interact with others so as to isolate and transpose those values onto a new model of gender relations, thereby promoting an epistemological rupture and profound social change. Darcy de Oliveira believes that the female culture and universe exist, that they are the expression of the social and historical experience of the female body and psyche and that their difference is manifested through their acceptance of the concept of approximation, not appropriation, as a model for change.

As an "other"—an outsider in Europe—Darcy de Oliveira's observations on the contributions and limitations of the European feminist movement add an interesting crosscultural perspective to the essay. This critical perspective is never so acute as when she considers the existence of a specifically feminine form of writing, or when she reflects upon the major figures of "écriture féminine," a movement most Americans know only through scattered English translations of select essays by French feminist writers of the 1970s and 1980s that have appeared in anthologies and academic journals. Not surprisingly, Darcy de Oliveira cautions against creating a standard, such as that prescribed by French feminists, which may once again make women who write differently feel inadequate.

In the chapter "The Madwomen of the Plaza de Mayo," Darcy de Oliveira comes back full-circle to her cultural roots in Latin America, where she discovers the modern-day

Antigones, the female political actors whose ancestral feminine values form the basis of a grassroots movement that has the power to transform our material reality in the twenty-first century. Her position regarding women's contemporary identity crisis is closely aligned with the project of ecofeminism where nature and the spiritual are significant not as essence but as experience. Thus, when she calls for the adoption of feminine values to create a human history of nature which would include, by extension, a history of feminism, or the feminine as history, she refers not so much to the absence of a concept as to one that has yet to take shape.

Darcy de Oliveira herself is well on the road to making this history. Her efforts at IDAC and at the National Council on Women's Rights to sponsor initiatives targeted at the grass roots organization of Brazilian women represent her own attempt to transform the feminine into politics. By involving those who have not traditionally had access to the decision-making process, Darcy de Oliveira reveals her vision of a new concept of power; not power in the name of equality but power in the name of difference. In a 1994 interview, she distinguished between two kinds of power: power not only defined in terms of politics but also in terms of culture through the capacity of being heard. Furthermore, she observed that women today "are not seeking power for power's sake but in the name of something else . . . in the name of the regeneration of the very concept of power."[3]

By engaging Brazilian women in the fight against hunger and in the struggle for access to better education and health care, Darcy de Oliveira seeks to circumvent the mistakes of the past by leading women into the public sphere without their becoming mired in the territory of the masculine. She wants the values of the ancestral feminine to be heard in the territory of the masculine; compassion and solidarity to win over individual interests; the feminine to transform the public sphere;

and, finally, the feminine to recreate itself. Yet, she rejects the notion that this project is idealist and, therefore, unattainable. To believe in democracy, she says, is to believe that the world is for everyone, not just for the privileged few. To make this vision a reality requires standing behind the belief that violence and hunger should be unacceptable to all socioeconomic classes. Darcy de Oliveira sees humankind at a crossroads of civilization and barbarism, and she believes that we need only reject hunger in order to get to the side of civilization.[4] Consequently the twenty-first century for her began with the international conference in Peking where women, collectively, made the decision to combat poverty above all else.

Darcy de Oliveira acknowledges that Brazilian women have gained much from the various local and state agencies which, over the past decade, have made significant strides in articulating their interests. Yet, she believes women must learn to take part in their own defense and have responsibilities to society as well.[5] As the chief administrator of the Council on Women's Rights, Darcy de Oliveira's principal objective is to involve women in a discourse of action, not victimization. An integral part of this discourse is the identification of women's most basic needs and the struggle against the things Brazilian women are no longer willing to tolerate under any circumstances. Under her skillful leadership, the Council on Women's Rights is bringing visibility to women's needs on the local, state, and national levels, as well as monitoring policy making.

Through her work as a public figure and intellectual, feminist scholar and leading proponent of the link between the feminine and the protection of the environment, Darcy de Oliveira continues to affect women world wide. Her ultimate goal is to support "[the] emergence of a feminine subject, endowed with self-awareness, science, desire, political resolve and ethical conviction, [which] will mean that the fight for equality that has marked the twentieth century will culminate and bear fruit, finally, in the culture of the twenty-first century, in recognition for and exercise of the difference. This difference will express itself to the extent that women are able to enrich the human history of nature, combating the scourges of our time—the disharmony of the earth, the sorrow of the people and life being led astray."[6]

The present translation may contribute to that wonderful enrichment envisioned by Darcy de Oliveira. It is my hope that *In Praise of Difference: The Emergence of a Global Feminism* will help close the gap that has prevented the rich intellectual tradition of Latin American dissident voices from becoming more familiar to an English-speaking audience. However, it was perhaps inevitable that many of the stylistic qualities that distinguish Darcy de Oliveira's writing in Portuguese would be lost in translation—*traduttore, traditore*. A word must therefore be said about some of the difficulties confronting the translator. Darcy de Oliveira's style, in common with much of the theoretical, critical writing tradition in the Romance tongues, abounds in lengthy sentences, complex syntax, numerous synonyms, nouns in apposition, and parenthetical phrases, multiple prepositional phrases, abundant dependent clauses, and the frequent use of simile and metaphor. Naturally, a direct rendering of this style would result in an ungainly, unnatural English. Darcy de Oliveira's syntax has proven to be this translator's greatest challenge. Hence, it was frequently necessary to simplify syntax, break up long sentences, and occasionally even omit certain redundancies. In some places I have combined a succession of short paragraphs into one longer paragraph. Another feature of theoretical prose in Portuguese, and other Romance languages, is the omission of transitional words. To render the text intelligible in English, it has occasionally been necessary to add such terms. Only where Darcy de

Oliveira's characteristic use of incomplete sentences led to a lack of clarity in English, complete sentences were created, usually through the addition of a verb. Beyond this, I have done everything possible to retain the flavor, tone, flow, and colorful qualities of the Brazilian writer's eloquent prose.

A word about the translation of quotations and the use of citations. Since Darcy de Oliveira relies on a theoretical bibliography of largely French works, I used published English translations of the original French sources wherever possible. Where English translations were unavailable, the translations are mine. Also, where Darcy de Oliveira synthesizes the work of others without citing specific passages from the original, I have, in some cases, used both French and English original sources to guide me in my translation. However, the bibliography remains by and large as it appeared in her original, with few exceptions, without the addition of the translations I employed.

In resolving some of the above-mentioned linguistic problems, I was able to call for assistance on my colleague Thomas C. Meehan, whose knowledge of language and experience with some of the challenges inherent in translation have helped to transform this project into a more rewarding learning experience for me. Finally, my sincere gratitude to Marlie Wasserman, director of Rutgers University Press, and Thomas Stephens of Rutgers University whose vision and appreciation of the significance of Brazilian intellectuals like Darcy de Oliveira made the English language version of this essay come to fruition. Their recommendation, encouragement, and whole-hearted support of this project are deeply appreciated.

University of Illinois at Urbana-Champaign
December 1997

In Praise of Difference

Introduction ✺ CHAPTER 1

No, I hadn't even been able to formulate the question. Nevertheless, the answer had continually posed itself to me since I was born. It had been because of that insistent answer that, in a reverse path, I had been forced to look for the question to which it corresponded.
Clarice Lispector[1]

This book is an attempt to approach the feminine. While tracking it down, it was possible, here and there, to map out boundaries. That's all.

In her introduction to *The Passion According to G.H.*, Clarice Lispector states that she would be happy if she were read by people "whose outlook is fully formed. People who know that an approach to anything whatsoever must be carried out gradually and laboriously, that it must traverse even the very opposite of what is being approached."[2] I learned with Clarice, who helped nurture my soul, and today I'm aware that moving toward the feminine requires crossing into the masculine. For women, this journey, with its multiple dimensions of estrangement and solitude, but also of adventure, enrichment, and enlightenment, was, and still is, a form of exile.

In the experience of exile, the obvious loses its naturalness and, in our encounter with the other, we discover, often to our surprise, that we are the other for someone else. We establish comparisons and analyze parts of ourselves that we never knew existed because we had never experienced being distanced from ourselves. No mirror reveals one's identity better than exile.

The incursion of women into the world of men, their entrance into that strange culture, the acquisition of new codes, permit the manifestation of incompatibilities which, like the edges of the pieces of a jigsaw puzzle, prevent that piece from being placed where it doesn't belong. It won't work to force it in and risk damaging it. Instead of imitation as the basis for equality, women today are seeking difference as their identity. Yet, the articulation of that difference is problematic, especially when the only recourse for expressing it is an arsenal of strange words and concepts, or when it must be expressed in a discourse that in itself is masculine.

It is not by chance that the first signs of the emergence of the feminine appeared somewhat timidly in turn-of-the-century literature, taking refuge in the realm of the imaginary where insubordinate fantasy goes beyond the description of the world as given and seeks to invent it. For women, literature was not a simple transgression of the unwritten laws prohibiting their access to creativity. Rather, it was a liberated, clandestine territory pulsating to the emotional rhythm of that secrecy and risk: a furtive outlet from the constraints of language and from the ideas that conceptualized and described them in absentia.

The era of art as a form of escape was followed by the challenge of science. For many women involvement with science represented a more serious transgression than their predecessors' ventures into fantasy. Women's unauthorized appropriation of the most precious instrument of masculine culture—intimacy with science—was possible then just as it is today, but only at the price of a strange ambiguity. Upon achieving the status of scientist, they discovered the fictional nature of science as a concept, they found out that it was just another fragile version of a world that teeters on the verge of its own dissolution. More surprises!

My generation inherited an age in which women lost more than they gained, an era in which suddenly, in the space of a lifetime, certainties that had lasted millennia collapsed before our very eyes, and we felt the ground shaking under our feet. It is for this very reason that we have to assume the responsibility for recreating the feminine. This comes at a time when women no longer recognize themselves in the lyrical images, lived experiences, and depictions that echo in the "eternal feminine" of the poets; when crossing into ambiguous terrain is the price they must pay for experiences they desire but fear, emptiness becomes their point of departure.

Women have attempted a border-crossing into the world of men, yet they surreptitiously dragged their domestic roots with them. They adopted masculine lifestyles, yet men weren't becoming more feminine at the same time. In response to society's schizophrenic command—be male and female at the same time—women occupied a middle ground as they tried to narrow the gap between two different lifestyles and ways of communicating. This is precisely how the dream of equality derailed; a man need only be a man, the norm, the standard by which women are measured, and to which women must be equal and different all at once.

But no one can be herself and the other at the same time. Far from the eternal feminine, beyond ambiguity, which is the only possible solution to contradictory messages, inventing the feminine requires the creation of a language that will allow women to express themselves without becoming trapped by the logic of definitions. From the point of view of masculine logic, to oppose this logic is tantamount to affirming its opposite through the use of the same words within the same frame of reference. The existence of an alternate logic—one in which approximating something not yet defined is preferable to appropriating a prefabricated identity in the image of man—is inconceivable. Approximating the feminine, inventing it day by day, is the direction women will take as the century draws to a close.

The feminine is no longer what it was, and it is no longer possible to define it as anything but a process of profound disorganization or, to use a cliché, of transformation. The traditional thought process that defined a concept through its opposite, by changing the sign, by inverting its characteristics, has broken down. Masculinity and femininity used to be defined by this mutually exclusive relationship that some benignly preferred to view as correlational. However, history is full of traps, and our era came face to face with men and women whose concerns, though unique, were unforeseeable in a past that was supposedly symmetrical. As women's social roles and experiences in the world began to change, they felt torn between the past and the future, between memory and desire.

Feminism planted its roots in this "no man's land." Like all social movements, it challenged the existing symbolic order that had for so long attributed to the masculine the right to define the feminine as its opposite. Today we are experiencing the disavowal of this traditional arrangement, a plunge into disorder which, paradoxically, has become the new organizing principle.

The more enlightened segments of society seem to have internalized the concept of sexual equality—the first stage of this transgression. Yet, the battle between the sexes appears to become more deeply rooted in society as new possibilities open up for women. A feminism of equality has become a feminism of difference, and it is at this juncture that understanding such a process becomes more complex. Could women be the victims of an outbreak of traditionalism? Could they be reinvesting in the past and be subscribing to ideas they have been combating for an entire century? Certainly not! Furthermore, it would be a grave error to equate a feminism of difference with the discriminatory gender ideology of the past.

Looking back is inscribed in the process of the search for identity. Women's identities cannot be separated from the daily social practices that constitute women's existence and shape what we might call a specifically female point of view—the result of their unique experience of being in the world. Female identity is a tributary to a feminine culture that has traditionally marked the existential experiences of all women.

The fact that this culture developed on the periphery of the masculine world and has served historically as a pretext for exclusion—as well as an alibi for confinement—does not negate its existence or invalidate the best of what was generated within its confines: familiarity with the sensual, the recognition that intuition is as valid as reason, the sense of what is close rather than what is one's own.

The feminism of difference draws its civilizing critique from the best of that other realm. The difficulty of understanding the process in which women are immersed lies precisely in capturing the dynamics by which they, basing themselves in their feminine experience, reject the limits imposed on them and invent themselves anew, closer now to the world of men but without dissolving in an undifferentiated magma; furthermore, this is being carried out with a critical potential inspired by their history.

It is not a question here, as one might think, of an essence that, submissive to nature and erroneously understood as unchangeable, immobilized history. Quite to the contrary, it is about breaking the anachronistic dichotomy between nature and culture and experiencing surprise in the middle of a "human history of nature." In the feminine, as in the masculine, the body is a historical experience. When women look to the past to recover their feminine culture, it is not the essence of the feminine that they seek, but rather the feminine as experience. Today, this past experience finds new ways of life and new demands, and it is in this process of change that the feminine is gradually taking on a different form.

The emergence of the feminine as a cultural paradigm has been going on without even pronouncing its name. It has been going on within an understanding of the world that is not content with the exclusive use of reason and does not recognize reason as all-powerful; it refuses to accept the body as a submissive instrument of production and attempts to win back its erotic dimensions. This has been expressed in the babbling of what is at times unintelligible language, constituted more of silences and listening than codified avowal. The feminine emerges as a force of alterity, an acknowledgment that there are different positions from which humankind can reflect on its experience, imagine itself otherwise, conceive itself differently, even if that difference seeks its vitality in what seems outdated. Perhaps this is the extraordinary dialectic of the present. In reframing human relations, we discover an extraordinary capital and an impressive wealth that is contained in those relations; and we bring this discovery up to date by placing it at the service of a project that uniquely articulates the relationships between the public and the private, the personal and the political.

The feminization of life involves reexamining the place of work in the daily lives of men and women, redefining the political, interrogating science and art from the perspective of deconstructing concepts, and inventing a language. Feminization is a continuous process, even though it has not been formally recognized as such and even though the mark of the feminine has not been identified in it.

When humanity finally becomes aware of the need to reestablish the dialogue with nature after its failed attempt to disengage from it or ignore it entirely, perhaps then the emerging feminine can mediate the renewal of this contact. In a time when reminding humanity of its natural dimension was considered reactionary and backward, identifying women as closer to nature meant diminishing them, placing them, in a certain sense, beyond the human which was monopolized by men, situating them on a lower plane of development which justified the need for surveillance and control. The inferior place women occupied in their relationships with men had, like cause and effect, as in perfect circularity, the identification by everyone—including women themselves—of the feminine with the bestial, with unbridled pursuit of pleasure, with an attendant threat to a principle of reality; this principle supposedly lies at the root of civilization from the standpoint of instinctive control and the primacy of reason.

The deconstruction of those convictions, which served as a foundation not only to the hierarchical relationship between the sexes, but also to the specific relationship each gender established with nature, has been accelerating as the end of the twentieth century approaches. The paradigmatic separation of nature and culture is entering a decline, the victim of its own successes, which are threatening to end in crushing failure. The ecological movements have been heralded by a vital necessity to rethink the history of man and his view of the earth. The presence of the natural in the human has come to be considered today not as a vestige of traditionalism but as a demand of modernity. This dialogue with nature presupposes an *aggiornamento*, which would seem easier for women who have distanced themselves less from nature.

The emergence of the feminine is a widespread symptom of our time as well as a conscious desire on the part of women, at least those women who place their faith in the contribution of the feminine to civilization. However, this desire holds practical risks. Women who have escaped the eternal feminine and no longer need to imitate men in the unsuspected pitfalls of life accept those risks. What they are attempting to live is not a crystallized essence, neither is it an immanence or a predestination. It is a continuum in which body, culture, history, and social status interact, and which comes accompanied by insertion and unusual configurations. What they are defending is a new kind of gender equality, the primacy of difference without hierarchy and without ambiguity.

Sometimes, when I reflect on the women's movement, the existential and intellectual effervescence it has generated, and the risks we are running, I am reminded of an Indian myth told by Henri Desroche. After carefully tying a loop at the end of a rope, a fakir throws the rope up into the sky and, certain that it has latched onto something beyond the clouds, he calmly climbs the rope. To the surprise of the incredulous people watching, he disappears into the sky, sure that the rope had caught onto—who knows what?—maybe his hope. Because hope is like that, seemingly illusory, but that illusion gradually impregnates and constitutes reality, like a vital force from within.

The women's movement was, and still is, for me and my generation, that rope which we are climbing to prove that there is a more tender, more gentle world within reach. And if there isn't, the fact that we have been able to envision such a world has already brought us closer, perhaps, to a more humble, but oh so precious objective—that of inaugurating a network of human relations in which the acceptance of difference without inequality reconciles men and women, thereby putting an end to women's misencounters with themselves.

Sexual Dichotomy and Inequality ❈ *CHAPTER 2*

Order is crystallized through the changing mass of virtual disorder.
　　　　　　　　　　Serge Moscovici

*Sisterhood is blooming;
springtime will never be the same.*
　Slogan of the Women's Liberation Movement
　　　　　　　　(United States, 1971)

❈ The Feminine as Political Crime

On the eve of her engagement to Haemon, the king's son, Antigone slips outside the palace walls of Thebes at dawn. Defying her uncle Creon's decree, she is on her way to burying her brother Polynices, Oedipus' rebellious son, who had been killed in battle during the attack of the seven foreign princes against Thebes, his native city. Each step her bare feet take on the plain before Thebes brings Antigone closer to her destiny and sets the gears of tragedy in motion. Her tragedy is the conflict between two causes, two truths, two logics. Sophocles' *Antigone* is the archetype of tragedy. The confrontation between Oedipus' daughter and her uncle, the king, reveals not only the inevitable conflict that opposes a woman to a man, or the demands of personal conscience to public duty, above all it reveals the contrast between the logic of the public space and the private space.

Creon is the master of the public space. Within that sphere, which is off-limits to women, reside the men who make and enforce the laws in the name of the state. However, when Creon invokes the interests of the city and forbids Polynices' burial, Antigone rebels. Antigone is unlike other women; she is Oedipus' daughter, "the savage daughter of a savage Father and King," born of transgression and condemned to transgress. When Antigone leaves the palace, she takes her sister Ismene with her. This first incursion of Antigone into secrecy precludes the possibility of any witnesses to the dialogue between the daughters of Oedipus. Antigone confronts Ismene with a choice that will determine whether her sister is loyal to her noble ancestry or whether she has lost her sense of nobility. Antigone believes that for her sister to prove herself a true descendant of Oedipus, Ismene must accompany her on the mission considered vital by Antigone: to bury her brother Polynices, victim of Eteocles' fratricide, both brothers having fallen in a dirty war of succession to the throne. With two sons dead, all that remains of Oedipus' lineage are two daughters.

Creon, who occupies the throne, sees Polynices as a traitor and Eteocles as a hero. Hence, Eteocles is to be buried with all due rites and thereby will secure his rightful place among the dead; Polynices, the traitor, is to become carrion, to be left to the vultures without mourning or funeral, a dead man without a grave, a soul condemned to suffer without ever finding repose. This is the king's decree, the law of the city, against which Antigone now rises up, determined to bury her brother and save his soul. But by doing so, she herself will face being condemned to death; by contrast, Ismene submits to those laws and decrees because they cannot be ignored and, furthermore, as she observes: "We must rather bear in mind, first that we are women, not meant to fight against men; then that we are ruled by those who are stronger, and so must obey in these things, and in things yet worse than these."[1]

To insist on such a transgression is to let oneself be seduced by the impossible. However, the impossible is precisely Antigone's objective, and here she is ready to commit a triple political crime: to transcend the walls of her home, the protected space of the feminine; to enter into the political arena by subverting the law; and, finally, to challenge not only the law of the state, which condemns her brother, but also the law of man, which condemns her, woman, to silence. Ismene is Antigone's opposite. Molded by society's norms, she submits and enunciates her consent with lowered eyes. Ismene's obedience is struck by the lightning of Antigone's dissent.

Ismene and Antigone represent two sides of the feminine, two possible viewpoints in the conflictive dialogue of the feminine with itself: either to accept the foundational laws that strictly separate the world of men from the world of women, subordinating the latter to the former; or to subvert that order by crossing the border between the domestic and the political.

Silent mourning would have better protected the uneasy and already condemned body lying on the field and moving toward its destiny. Unfortunately, Antigone chose to leave behind the security of the feminine, the comfort of a repetitious, approved, applauded, and expected behavior. Outside, beyond the limits of her home, a greater, more inevitable, more fatal conflict awaits Antigone. Before her now rises her uncle, the king, a man.

Enter Creon to play out his role. The first words of his speech to the citizens of Thebes, his political platform, categorically affirm the primacy of the public over the private; they denounce family loyalty which would place the common good at risk. The spectacle of his nephew's body left to the vultures can only be justified by unwavering certainty that he is in power to maintain the law against everything and everybody, and especially against the temptation of an emotional appeal that would arouse and weaken the integrity of the polis.

That certainty is woven of the same threads that will weave the web into which both Creon and Antigone will fall without possibility of salvation. A few more minutes into the play and we have before us a disheveled girl with nails full of dirt, being dragged by her hair like a common criminal, an insolent princess who escaped her home and her future on the eve of becoming the wife of the king's son and, later, the mother of his grandchildren.

Face to face, these dramatic characters play out the irreconcilable conflict of opposites, of different natures, and the confrontation between the logic of the masculine and the logic of the feminine which throughout human history have remained so radically foreign to each other. A victory by Antigone would topple Creon from his privileged masculine position: "This girl was already well versed in insolence when she transgressed the laws which had been laid down; and, when she had so acted, here was further insolence, to boast of these things and exult at having done them. Now I swear that she is a man and I am not, if she is to prevail in this and go unpunished."[2]

Antigone knows she was born to love and not to hate, and nothing would be able to console her were she to leave a body born of her mother without a grave. She also knows that the laws she is challenging are less important than others that have been in force since the beginning of time and which nobody recorded because they were promulgated by the gods. Anarchy: isn't that uncontested power?

For there is no greater evil than disobedience: it is this that destroys cities, this that makes houses desolate, this that breaks up allied ranks in rout. But when men succeed, it is obedience that most often saves their lives.

Thus the appointed rules must be upheld, and we must on no account be beaten by a woman. Better to fall from power, if fall we must, before a man; and at least we would not be called *women's* inferiors.[3]

Inadmissible inversion of the rules of the world. Emergence of a different logic, an alternative to common sense, which will be the stuff of tragedy. The only recourse against the logic in question is murder or suicide. For logic is not only an expression of discretionary power, it is convinced of its own correctness as well.

The death of Antigone does not save Creon from the new conflict awaiting him. His son Haemon now arrives on the scene, afflicted, in despair over Antigone's fate, a young prospective groom deprived of his bride on the eve of his wedding. Here the logic of the masculine collides with another version of the masculine. Just as Ismene appeared at the beginning of the play as a peacemaking voice in the conflict, now it is Haemon's turn to offer his father a sweeter, more flexible version of a king, one who is less absolute in his judgments, less certain of a singular truth. Haemon suggests to Creon the image of certain trees in a windstorm which know how to bend and thereby save their fragile branches while the more rigid ones end up being uprooted. A heart capable of going back on its hatred, of giving in to tenderness, would be the guarantee of a more fertile existence and of better government. However, Creon, like Antigone, exists as a symbol of the absolute. In the king's eyes, Haemon has allied himself with women, has ceased being a man, and has been enslaved by women, thus becoming a plaything of the enemy and the spokesman of an unintelligible language.

Haemon, a diluted version of the masculine; Ismene, a diluted version of the feminine: both are accomplices in the tragedy of Creon and Antigone, the most autonomous characters in the literature of classical antiquity. Autonomous in the true sense of the word: those possessing their own law. They are necessary to each other, one is the inverted image of the other, the other of the other, each immersed in the same obsessive passion of implacably fulfilling a destiny. Like paradoxical mirrors, Antigone and Creon reflect, on stage, a nonnegotiable sexual dissimilarity of both strangeness and enchantment. The masculine and the feminine converse in contradictory fashion with each other. Antigone speaks with her body, her center is outside of time, her temporality is ageless; she is familiar, therefore, with the world of the dead, the before and the after that involve transcendence. Creon is contingent upon the here and now; his temporality is historical. He speaks with the logic that politics arrogates to itself.

Creon prevents the power of time from playing with the living and the dead. If Polynices' body was refused the shelter of the earth, Antigone, paradoxically, will be buried alive. Her final lament on the last day of her life turns to the woman's destiny she could have had but did not have, and at the moment of death we see her only moment of weakness. She laments her lost marital happiness, the children she will never bear, the song of Hymen she will never hear, and she addresses the dead:

> From what parents was I born, their wretched daughter! To them I go thus, accursed, unwedded, to share their home....
>
> Such was the law by which I singled you out for honour; but to Creon I seemed to be doing wrong in this and acting as a reckless criminal, my own brother....
>
> And now he leads me like this, a prisoner in his hands, deprived of bridal bed and wedding song, having had no por-

tion of marriage or the raising of children; instead I go thus, unhappy one, bereft of friends, alive to the hollow place of the dead. And what divine law have I transgressed?[4]

However, Antigone's weakness is only momentary. There is no other fear in that spirit that sought not temporal power but the respect for nature that links human beings beyond life and death, beyond time and history; the feminality that mourns the loss, in life, of the woman, the mother, and the wife. Antigone's grandeur as a dramatic character also derives from this immense weakness that invades her at the hour of her death; it is not remorse, but a profound sense of tragedy that touches her as it crushes her tenderness.

While Antigone, deprived of her clarity of vision, voices her lament, the gloom of an evil omen now descends upon Creon. Tiresias' prophecy is implacable; before sundown, Creon will pay with the blood of his blood, with the death of his son, with Antigone's sacrifice, and with the desecration of Polynices' body. The dénouement is well known: Creon tries to turn back and, by saving Antigone, prevent the pain from spreading and contaminating everything and everybody. Too late, for Antigone has already taken her life; Haemon kills himself in front of his father, and Eurydice, Creon's wife, unconsoled over her son's suicide, joins him in death. The lament, an invocation of death, anticipated, desired, and urgent, is now up to Creon, as earlier it was up to Antigone, because that invocation represents his fated reunion with his loved ones. Temporal power, defeated and humiliated, now dissolves into the hope for infinite time.

Thus, Antigone and Creon become prisoners of their own truths. There is no way out of the conflict that places them in opposition to each other. Their respective forms of logic negate and exclude each other with no possibility for negotiation. Antigone cannot and will not give in. Her actions condemn her.

Creon can only repeat the sentence already uttered in the prohibition that Antigone chose to transgress. If Antigone must challenge Creon to fulfill her destiny, for him, the king, a man, her actions are madness, insanity, disorder which lead to chaos. Both will be punished, but the law of man will remain the law of society. Condemned to perpetual exile, guilty of invading the territory of men with the logic of the feminine, Antigone is banished from the world of the living without finding shelter or repose even in the realm of the dead. Not even the daughter of Oedipus can subvert the world order with impunity.

Antigone's myth echoes through time, an unceasing voice persistently repeating its message. Born or imagined in human fantasy, it reverberates, as in a recurring dream, with fundamental representations of our sexual identity. As George Steiner explains, like Oedipus, Electra, Prometheus, or Icarus, Antigone as a mythical figure is a "collective personification" and her confrontation with Creon stages a primordial psychosocial conflict: the segregation of men and women into separate physical and psychic territories which are asymmetrical and complementary.[5]

Just like hand prints found in the depths of caves or like temples erected on hillsides to the glory of the gods, myths are testimonies to the human phenomenon. They are waves of the collective unconscious that break on the shores of the centuries; they always reach us in the same form but reinvented. They awaken contradictory feelings, a kind of memory of what has already been lived—hence recognizable—but they also create the surprise of the uncommon. Myths are made of the present and the past. Antigone is one of those myths, perhaps the most persistent, that has touched generations with its captivating force, invoking identifications, serving as a metaphor for irreconcilable opposites. Each generation visits the story of Antigone with the anguish of its own conflicts and finds in it a mirror filled with the images and phantoms of its own age. From Goethe to Brecht, Western thought has immersed itself in Sophocles' tragedy and has dramatized in each period its own conflict through the confrontation between a rebellious young princess and a headstrong old king in order to evoke the discord between private conscience and public law.

To revisit Antigone at the end of the twentieth century is to fulfill the destiny of Western thought which, in agreement with or rejection of that transgression, lives out its eternal return in the tragedies of antiquity. Sophocles' tragedy reflects multiple ontological oppositions: between youth and old age; between the living and the dead. The confrontation between men and women—the unavoidable conflict between the contiguous yet contradictory worlds of the feminine and the masculine—is brought up to date at the end of the twentieth century. Meanwhile, the embers of feminism are still warming our social environment which has become unrecognizable in the wake of the breakdown of the ancestral paradigm that had separated the world of men from that of women.

In the evocation of Antigone echoes the nonconformity of generations of women who in the last twenty years have finally rejected the decree of absence and silence that excluded them from politics. They have challenged social condemnation and have taken their first uncertain steps into the territories of the masculine. That echo has become increasingly audible as women seek—following their first attempts to be heard through their simple presence and eloquence—to employ the logic of the feminine in the realm of the political by means of their presence and voice.

During the earlier years of feminism, women employed the logic of the masculine as if it were a foreign language in order to make themselves better understood in the public sphere. Even then they encountered resistance and a lack of understanding that seemed unjust and exclusionary to them. Today the tone in the uneven dialogue between men and women is changing. The feminine voice evolved from the modest ambition of simply making itself heard in the public sphere to the articulation of a new logic of the feminine which is now much more abrasive and infinitely more subversive. The feminine voice thus dramatizes once again Antigone's challenge to Creon in a modern confrontation. Women today are discovering an archetypal face in Antigone's mirror where so many would recognize their own reflection. In times of unavoidable conflict, the fragile Theban princess stands alone in her naked femininity and affirms her own law, thus contradicting the masculine authority of both king and man. Recalled to life once again, drawn from oblivion, she returns to center stage and beckons new generations of women.

❋ The Separation of Worlds: Thoughts, Words, and Deeds

Motivated by our contemporary problems, we read Antigone as a discourse on the age-old question of gender differences and discover that our reading now enjoys the support of modern anthropology. This discipline has discovered the refrain of sexual difference as the very foundation of culture in the fantastic diversity of human societies as well as in the countless ways human beings organize themselves and conduct their relationships.

Gender differences are mirrored and abound in every area of our individual experience. The modeling of each gender's specific image and role, quite independent of the logic that accompanies it, confirms the principle of separation and difference in every society examined.[6] Although motivated differently, masculine and feminine have consistently made their presence felt. No culture has dared to dilute them into human sameness. It matters little that the content of each of these two worlds varies; a distinct "sexual duality" remains intact, a duality that numerous myths reaffirm in symbolic language and which Georges Balandier has characterized as the "paradigm of all paradigms."

The cultural and social universe of mankind is organized around the axis of gender dichotomy. Each pole is associated with specific features and qualities that reflect differences and complementary attributes: hot/cold, hard/soft, day/night, sun/moon, strength/fertility, war/fecundity, order/disorder, active/passive, superior/inferior, and so on. The "order of life" is founded upon that opposition between the sexes, upon that "law of dynamic union of differences and contradictions." Even though that law is so generalized and so powerful that it takes on the guise of a universal law of human nature, it is still perceived as uncertain and vulnerable by humankind.

In the masculine imagination, women are not only perceived as different but mainly as inferior. Hence, it is paradoxical to depict women as "the dangerous half of society." As bearers of the earth's fertility and of the fecundity of the human species, women are perceived as closer to primitive nature than to the "human landscape." Yet, there emanates from them the supreme threat that, if they break the primordial relationship of alterity/opposition and reject men, the soil will dry up and the species will be annihilated: "Due to their position of alterity, women are defined as dangerous and the antagonist. In light of this adversarial relationship, they are frequently associated with the forces of change which corrode the social order and established culture."[7]

For men, women are, above all else, the other, an other, much more than just a companion. That strangeness is expressed and feeds upon the symbolic and representational systems, thereby reinforcing the fixed barriers separating the actions and knowledge of men and women. The mapping of that archaic, untouchable border goes right along with philogyny. Yet, the clarity of the map's lines are lost at the point where hunting and gathering, upon being differentiated, transform biosocial differences into differences of being in the world, just as among the primates. Each gender specializes in a specific relationship with its environment. Furthermore, that specialization transforms each gender's relationship with its environment as well as with the other gender. There is a world of men and a world of women which exist side by side, yet unable to communicate, and their characteristic features become ever more distinct: "Masculine and feminine each develops its own sociability, its own culture, its own psychology. This psychocultural difference is reinforced, and in turn it makes the physical-endocrinous difference more complex."[8]

From generation to generation, each gender, committed to one and only one aspect of reality, reaffirms the coexistence of two worlds, constructed separately and sustained by practices that are foreign to the other. Considering all aspects of human existence—space, work, shelter, language, food, myth, and magic—gender dichotomy is the unmistakable experience of doing and knowing. This reproduces the links with a specific facet of the environment since the environment is much more than a passive storehouse of natural resources that men explore in their effort to survive.

> This environment is the place where objects and supplies can be found. But it is also a book written by successive generations, recording the migrations of populations, their influence on the distribution of animals and plants, and the way in which climate, watercourses and mountains have determined the choice of routes or settlements. It must be deciphered and in-

ternalized by the children of the species, together with the ancestral divisions of night and day and the seasons of the year, with their related activities.⁹

Upon reproducing itself, society actually duplicates the differences between its two halves, thereby specifying the relationship of each half to the environment. The verification of the coexistence of the territories of the masculine and the feminine imposes itself as evidence of that coexistence. Even more obscure is the origin of the hierarchy that designates political and social authority to the masculine as it imposes its model on all dimensions of human relations. In his attempt to illuminate that shadowy zone, Edgar Morin suggests that the affirmation of masculine superiority coincides with the birth of the family as a microstructure of society:

> The family is a subsystem open to the social system. The father-husband belongs to the class of men, the mother-wife to the group of women, the child, beyond a certain age, to the group of uninitiated youth. Through that opening, the family will articulate with society by means of the organization of kinship and the regulation of sexuality. These will be linked through the institution of exogamy to a new opening of that same society with other allied societies wherein there exists the elaboration of a macrosocial metasystem.¹⁰

This social process toward ever greater complexity is closely linked with the broadening and deepening of masculine power, especially through the incest taboo, a phenomenon that, together with sexual dichotomy, enjoys the privilege of universality in human societies. As "the fundamental principle of culture," the incest taboo regulates the social distribution of the rare treasure which women represent and establishes—

through a system of barter between men, in which women become objects of exchange—the conditions of an alliance between men founded upon patriarchal power. The rules of kinship and marriage thus reveal their profound significance as structures of domination:

> The total relationship of exchange which constitutes marriage is not established between a man and a woman, where each owes and receives something, but between two groups of men, and the woman figures only as one of the objects in the exchange, not as one of the partners between whom the exchange takes place . . . the relationship of reciprocity which is the basis of marriage is not established between men and women, but between men by means of women, who are merely the occasion of this relationship.[11]

Dictated by the law of exogamy and by the incest taboo, the laws of marriage form the basic asymmetrical social relationship between the sexes. A man can only obtain a woman from another man. For men, the exchange of women is a gift that prompts a gift in return. This creates a social link between men, a system of alliances founded on reciprocity. For women, on the other hand, the exchange brings with it their reduction to the status of object; they are nothing more than the coin of exchange, signs and emblems of the dominant status of men.

Serge Moscovici, describing and interpreting the process of separation and hierarchy between the sexes, reinforces this idea:

> The world of men and the world of women circle in different orbits and in opposite directions. Men inhabit a universe of signs and women a universe of significance. Men achieve a marriage through alliance and for them kinship is a means:

women achieve alliance through marriage and kinship is their purpose. If the prohibition of incest marks the transition from nature to culture, it is a transition from a state of male and female equality to a state of male dominance. The prohibition, like all forms of social intervention, creates a dual set of relationships: reciprocity for the men and subordination for the women, the second being one of the conditions for the first.[12]

Discrimination and inequality, established by the rules of kinship and sexual dichotomy, divide society into two halves. That hierarchical dualism penetrates and permeates all dimensions of life and determines a differentiated process of transmission and acquisition of knowledge, values, and patterns of behavior. Each segment of society is associated with a part of the real through a game of erected barriers and proclaimed prohibitions. These are the borders of society's intellectual and practical horizons which guarantee the preservation of the specificity of roles and power. From the moment of birth, gender determines the individual's place on one side or the other of the border, the first selection that will be reinforced by social practice.

If marriage seals the alliance and complicity between men through women, it will be the role of the initiation to ritualize and confirm the domination of men over women through the male child. The fundamental objective of the numerous rites of passage practiced by human societies is precisely that of distancing the boy from the mother, substituting a community of men for her. To initiate a child means to define its gender. Identifying with other men, affirming his masculinity, the young male breaks his ties with childhood and with the feminine world. He experiences a second birth, a social birth through which he is incorporated as a legitimate member into the community of men. More than anything else, the initiation is the process of forgetting childhood, which is associated with the feminine; it is the forgetting of what has been lived and learned alongside women through a series of tests which the young boy must successfully pass to be admitted into adulthood associated with the masculine: "That passage is inseparable from a certain violence in actions and words. Gestures and rituals, songs and mimicry, represent the struggle of men against women; men win that struggle and assert their primacy, which indicates clearly the doctrinary character of the initiation."[13]

In the initiation, it is the task of men to take the male child away from the world of women, isolate him in a sacred and hidden place, on the margins of society, where, exposed to suffering and pain, the boy will prove his virility. That test takes on the guise of a symbolic death, the death of the child who used to belong to the world of women and who, through the experience of pain and the revelation of the mystery, will be reborn as an adult male. The test is personal and individual, but the staging is social and collective. By distancing young boys from women and commanding the rites of passage, men assert three powers at one and the same time: their domination over women; the superiority of adults over the young; and the split between the world of men and the world of women.

> The basic theme of the initiatory cult, however, is that women, by virtue of their ability to make children, hold the secrets of life. Men's role is uncertain, undefined, and perhaps unnecessary. By a great effort man has hit upon a method of compensating himself for his basic inferiority . . . they can get the male children away from the women, brand them as incomplete, and themselves turn boys into men. Women, it is true, make human beings but only men can make men.[14]

The construction of the sexual identity of boys demands the repression of the feminality acquired in their association with women, relegates the maternal to oblivion, and requires the renunciation of the traits of that feminine world into which they were absorbed as infants. According to Badinter, "Fear of the Other, coupled with fear of the Same, explains the conflict dualism of the sexes psychologically. This dualism reinforces the sense of gender identity and justifies the repression of the Other, objectively in social relations, and subjectively inside oneself."[15] Everything in the initiation confirms the "terrible threat" created by the confusion of the genders, by the lack of sexual differentiation, and by the erasure of the barriers that limit the feminine and the masculine.

In his psychological reading, George Lapassade questions the sociological interpretation of the initiation which emphasizes its significance as preparation for maturity and for the world of social rules. He examines it from the opposite point of view, seeing it as a prohibition of childhood and repression of uncontrollable desires. Thus, he opposes Durkheim, for whom the ritual is primarily a "school of social morality" which allows man to dominate his nature and create society within himself, thus internalizing, according to Reik, its norms and rules. For the latter, the hidden meaning of the rite of passage is the prohibition of the fundamental primitive desires of children: incest and parricide. "The initiation thus establishes a cultural order in which the initial disorder of desire is subjected to the laws of men."[16]

The readings of the phenomenon of initiation are multiple but their profound meaning revolves around a common axis. Whether the initiation exorcises the part of the feminine that each young male carries within him in order to confirm him in his virility; whether it serves to take the child away from the mother and link him to the world of men; whether it makes the young boy forget the time of domestic innocence and his experience in the world of women; whether it represents for the initiate a form of social rebirth after his own biological birth; whether it marks the repression of desires that were forbidden in childhood and his insertion into society with the acceptance of its laws and obligations; whether it sanctions the transition from nature to culture, from the private to the public sphere; finally, whether it privileges in each society one or several of those meanings, it always reaffirms a fundamental polarity: the feminine is associated with childhood and the natural, the masculine with adulthood and the social.

The feminine and the masculine oppose and contradict each other. Mixed with and assimilated into the world of children, women are relegated to the alien part of society, the part closest to nature with its wild, irrational vibrations, the subaltern and dangerous half that should be confined to a restricted and controlled space. Women's exclusion from the adult world is implicit in that split between the masculine and the feminine, in that unequal division. Women are lumped together with children, thus causing a slippage by which the feminine becomes childlike while men are defined by the attributes and objectives common to adulthood: chiefs, warriors, hunters, priests, it is the men who create the rules and values that ground culture and society.

In the multiple meanings of the initiation rites that mark the threshold of adulthood, the price of becoming a man is the renunciation of the feminine world wherein reside the nostalgic memory of childish pleasure and the undifferentiated belonging to the maternal. To constitute one's self as a man means that a boy must accept that separation by forgetting and renouncing, thereby sharing the destiny of his ancestors who, at that same price, constructed the rules and social norms.

The memory of the maternal body, associated with pleasure, is the greatest threat to the maturation process by which a boy abandons childhood to enter the world of men. Consequently, women, who cannot separate themselves from their bodies and who renew with each pregnancy the same experience of fusion with the child, are condemned to exclusion from the adult world by masculine logic. Women carry within them, inscribed in the body, the indelible mark of subversion of the foundation of the adult and masculine world, the very principle of reality.

Maternity, which could serve as a line of demarcation between childhood and adulthood of women, actually has that meaning blurred since maternity inhabits a shadowy zone. The experience of maternity does not bear within itself a movement of separation from a visceral link, rather, it reenacts outside the womb the visceral nature of that link. Maternity is nurtured by feelings of protection and communion while male initiation seeks separation and collaboration.

Maternity prolongs the natural, while initiation lays the foundation for the social through the establishment of law. It is that inherent subversion of the mother-child relationship that instills in men a feeling of fear and uneasiness vis-à-vis the feminine. The feminine is experienced as an appeal that cannot be echoed, as an unacknowledged nostalgia, as an irreversible past, but one that threatens to interject itself into the present. The male point of view transforms the adult woman into a paradox.

Women in the World of Men: Dis-ease, Divergence, and Conflict

The destiny of every cultural thrust is the shaping of the world according to its own creative talent, the unveiling of the mystery of life, a challenge to the fatality of death. Human culture bears the stamp of insatiable desire: a break with nature, a negation of the limits of fragile meanings, nonconformity vis-à-vis the darkness that science, like a burning candle, reveals in its amplitude more than it illuminates.

Tirelessly interrogating themselves about their relationship with the universe, men invented gods, made themselves into gods, destroyed those gods, destroyed themselves in their zeal to distinguish themselves from the routine of nature and to establish themselves as subjects before nature, yet outside of it. This position of exteriority to nature gave rise to and legitimized man's presumed self-image as predator. The environment—or "objective nature" as Jacques Monod has expressed it—exposed to man's manipulation, is experienced by them as an object to be transformed, obedient to the human desire for violation.

Meanwhile, a shadowy zone seemed to separate itself from that destiny of movement like a sacred territory recalcitrant to change. The feminine, its ancestral rhythms and gestures, the eternal feminine of the poets, a memory common to all men, fused with nature, enveloped in a uniform passivity that human culture, which was now called masculine, curiously refused to activate. That masculine culture encouraged representations of women as amphibious beings, more instinctive than men: alien to reason, rebellious to domestication, as if in them nature held on to its rights to permanence, immutability, and regularity. Like nature, women were not incorporated or considered significant to human/masculine culture. The confinement of the female sex in a limited relationship with scarcely a few aspects of the environment, a result of sexual differentiation, was now translated into an inequality of status and power. That confinement became a hierarchy which, owing to its unchanging quality, came to be perceived as a given of human behavior, inscribed in the body and dictated by it. Mythological and ideological representations only confirmed it.

Permanence and regularity have always ruled feminine existence, legitimized in the name of natural decrees which served as an explanation for the relationship of power and hierarchy in which women represent the dominated pole. It is against the backdrop of that domination that the human constructs itself in opposition to nature, while the feminine constructs itself as the assimilation of women into nature. That decree of immutability weighed on women, constituting itself into a blind spot in the spectacular endless combat which human culture presented to the determinisms and limitations of its biology.

However, the twentieth century prepared a surprise for that immutability. In the 1970s, the biologist Odette Thibault noted the inherent pitfall in all explanations of the relationships of domination between men and women which were restricted to the determination of the sociocultural through the biological. Thibault observes:

> If, when dealing with women, the topic of biology seems dangerous, it is because in the past, and even today, there are those who invoke a pre-established and fixed "essence" to define feminality, thus justifying the difference in status between the masculine and feminine. In this sense, one could say, paraphrasing Freud, that for women "biology is destiny." But "becoming" is precisely the privilege of the human species—both women and men.[17]

Now then, it is that becoming, that "human history of nature," which the twentieth century has come to reveal in all its complexity. Nature and culture, as never before, finally discovered their insoluble solidarity, their implacable interrelatedness, their common destiny.

The "constructions" which science and technology have generated regarding objective nature and its consequences; the growing human consciousness of belonging to nature vis-à-vis those consequences; the dimension of "artifact" which science, and medicine in particular, has added to the human body, all these factors have come together in the emergence of the idea of a culturalized nature and a natural culture. The old nature/culture dichotomy has been superseded by a new worldview in which the human being has become an integral part of nature. We are creating successive links with the environment and with the body which will transform humankind as well as nature and culture. Ultimately, this process is one and the same. Today we find ourselves committed to a natural contract rather than a social contract. We are now contemporaries of a revolution that is bringing about a new pact between culture and nature, a revolution that reverberates in the renovation of yet another pact, that of science with the social. It is in this new pact where women, above all, are at risk.

In the course of the twentieth century, science launched an assault on the immutability of the feminine. The discovery of contraception introduced cultural freedom where before there was only natural inevitability. Contraception allowed women to separate pleasure from procreation for the first time in history and, at the same time, allowed them to experience the culturalization of nature in the womb. That space which opened up in feminine existence shook the entire edifice of gender relationships. The social and moral consequences of the generalized practice of contraception would introduce in the feminine spirit the most subversive of convictions: the idea that our bodies belong to us. The liberation of women's pleasure and desire constitutes a pivotal point in women's history, an opening that had been coming about, somewhat imperceptibly, ever since the eighteenth century.

The interrogation of something so fundamentally archaic as the sexual hierarchy cannot be reconstituted through explanatory schemes linking cause and effect. There has been a merger of technical innovations and relations of production, scientific discoveries and technological changes, important transformations in the fields of sociocultural reference as well as the emergence of new aspirations, values, and forms of behavior, all of which have led to the continuing entrance of women into the public sphere.

An egocentric sociology or a simplistic view of the economy has tried to claim credit for the progressive erasure of the boundaries between the masculine and the feminine. However, in reality there are numerous factors that act on each other and create a process of disorganization of the traditional relationship between the sexes; or, seen from another point of view, these factors create a new, unpredictable, unthinkable, and, therefore, threatening organization.

Imprisoned within the strict limits of domestic space and confined to traditional female duties, or integrated into the lower end of the work force through the creation of new modes of production that emerge with the Industrial Revolution, women continue to occupy an "interior" and/or "inferior" social status.[18] Access to the world of paid employment was not a voluntary choice for women, nor did it lead them to greater independence and a better social position. It was poverty that pushed them into the factories where they had no choice but to perform the most difficult and poorly paid jobs.

Simultaneously, at the other end of the social hierarchy, more enlightened women took pride in rivaling men in refinement of spirit. In the velvety world of the salons, this became a tentative precursor of subsequent protests against the gap between the enlightened discourse of an upwardly mobile bourgeoisie in favor of equal rights among all citizens and the everyday reality that kept women, even those of the upper social strata, in a state of submission and dependence. Molière's success with *Les femmes savantes* and *Les précieuses ridicules* in the seventeenth century could not hold back an era in haste to bring about a new world. In the eighteenth century, *The*

Vindication of the Rights of Woman by Mary Wollstonecraft coexists with Sophie who, born of Émile's rib, had the kitchen as her horizon. Rousseau and Germaine Necker's quibbling over gender relations did not stop a certain Madame de Staël from ignoring Sophie and giving birth to *Corinne*.

That debate, coming from the top, was to be prolonged and amplified in the second half of the nineteenth century in a vindication of equality between the sexes at the level of political institutions and civil rights. In parallel fashion, at the bottom of society, the exploitation of the female workforce brings with it a growing participation of women in the struggles to improve working conditions despite the prejudice of male workers and unionists who were concerned just as much with preserving masculine supremacy in the bosom of the family as with prohibiting women's access to the factory. Their basic argument was that women constituted a cheap, disorganized, reserve industrial army easily manipulated by the factory owners. In fact, upon creating a feminine workforce, the Industrial Revolution introduced a first crack in the paradigmatic differentiation of worlds insofar as it separated the home from the workplace, and men and women now faced the same machines, rhythms, and demands of factory production.

The suffragettes mobilized the masses of women around their demand for the right to vote. At the same time they were faced with the cruelty of ridicule that was heaped upon them and the concealed crude violence awaiting them in the streets. Their invasion of the *polis*, the political space until then the exclusive territory of men, broke a second taboo in the hierarchical separation of the sexes. In the first decades of the twentieth century, the right to vote was gradually conceded to women, but that formal triumph did not change their subaltern position in any extensive way. For women like Rosa Luxemburg, who were actively engaged in the social struggles of their time, the liberation of women presupposed the liberation of humanity. Likewise, for the militants of emergent socialism, gender equality was understood as equality among all people; the class conflict had primacy over the hierarchy of the sexes, and the particular was dissolved in the universal.

Contemporary witnesses of that feverish struggle for equality, the voices of an almost inaudible minority, denounced the discrimination that penetrated more deeply, beyond the struggle for civil rights or the battle against material exploitation. Against the parameters of political and social equality with men, understood by the suffragettes as the standard and ideal of the human, these minority voices pitched their protest which rested on the singularity of women's interior space, thereby asserting the feminine as a specific outlook on the world.

In her analysis of feminine literature, Virginia Woolf sketches out that line of thought and, in her famous lectures at Giron College, she plants the seed of an idea that would only bear fruit fifty years later: the importance of "difference" in the debate over equality. Wondering about the influence of gender on the integrity of a novelist, "that integrity which I take to be the backbone of the writer," Woolf observes:

> But it is obvious that the values of women differ very often from the values which have been made by the other sex; naturally, this is so. Yet it is the masculine values that prevail. Speaking crudely, football and sport are "important"; the worship of fashion, the buying of clothes "trivial." And these values are inevitably transferred from life to fiction. This is an important book, the critic assumes, because it deals with war. This is an insignificant book because it deals with the feelings of women in a drawing-room. A scene in a battlefield is more important than a scene in a shop—everywhere and much more subtly the difference of value persists. The whole structure,

therefore, of the early nineteenth-century novel was raised, if one was a woman, by a mind which was slightly pulled from the straight, and made to alter its clear vision in deference to external authority. . . . But how impossible it must have been for them not to budge either to the right or to the left. What genius, what integrity it must have required in face of all that criticism, in the midst of that purely patriarchal society, to hold fast to the thing as they saw it without shrinking. Only Jane Austen did it and Emily Brontë. . . . They wrote as women write, not as men write.[19]

Meanwhile, the search for that psychic space of freedom, that "room of her own," will be revealed as something just as fleeting and illusory as the hopes placed in the revolutionary utopia.

It sometimes happens that one has been right all along, or that one does not have the means to reach one's ends. If individual rebellion, a minority of `one, is condemned to wither through isolation and stigmatization, collective movements can also fail due to the wrong strategy. Neither equality with men—as a result of the establishment of socialism—nor the feminine as its own, and therefore critical point of view, took root at the beginning of the century. The foundations of feminine oppression will, in fact, be weakened by the massive entrance of women into the public sphere and by the end of the control of female sexuality by men, which happens only in advanced industrial societies.

The incursion of women as protagonists onto the political, social, and cultural stage is inscribed within the framework of a broader change, a true crisis of civilization. Toward the end of the 1960s, this crisis weakened the principles and values that guarantee social order and the ideological consensus in Western industrial societies. The egalitarian impulse—awakened by the struggles against racial discrimination and colonial rule, the questioning of established knowledge, scientific reason, and institutionalized politics, the search for a "new magic" in the world and for some vitality in reaction to the uniformity and enormity of postindustrial society, the appearance of the ecological question—all these aspirations for a different life, a different world, right "here and now," converged to open a new breach in the foundations of society. Fissures and ruptures appeared where once there had been only passivity, conformity, and material prosperity.

L'esprit du temps is ripe for change. The limits of the possible are stretched. What is profoundly problematized, within the very bosom of Western society, is the model, until then implicit and unchallenged, of white, Western, adult, male superiority. In truth, it is the hierarchical paradigm that is being attacked through the questioning of one of its most ancient and most solid foundations: men's domination over women.

The massive entrance of educated women into the labor market and the devaluation of domestic life contributed powerfully to the destruction of the barrier between the private and the public, between the feminine and the masculine. It also contributed to the disintegration of a traditional female identity centered in the idea of a woman who felt fulfilled by the chores and concerns of home and hearth. The industrial foundations of society incited women to leave the home, to displace their desire for fulfillment to other planes, and contest their isolation within the sphere of the family. Throughout the 1960s women invested in the public space.

However, it is precisely through this attempt to integrate themselves into the world of men, on an equal footing with men, that women were to run up against obstacles that would transform the demand for equality into a trap that would end up placing their psychosocial identity in crisis. Erikson's concept of psychosocial identity attempts to bring about a synthesis between the components of psychological and sociological order which enter into the definition of personality inserted into its social context.[20] M. Zavalloni observes: "Identity is linked to the group as synthetic mediation between the individual essence and the essence of a common culture. . . . The nature of a specific identity, far from being the result of a universal consensus, constitutes, on the contrary, the privileged place of the expression of the ideological conflicts characteristic of a society."[21]

In an effort to adjust to the new profile that crystallized out of the break with their old identity, women find themselves in the position of having to reconcile two different lifestyles, two different intellectual and affective registers, two models of daily conduct. Defined by a norm and a model that is imposed on them, they have to accept the paradox of the universal and the particular placed upon them by a society that universalizes them as producers and differentiates them as women. Split by the inner conflict of belonging at one and the same time to the private sphere, the world of the home and family governed by emotions, feelings, and the affective, and to the public sphere, the world of work ruled by aggressiveness, competition, and the notion of productivity, women have discovered that access to masculine roles does not necessarily guarantee equality, and that equality, understood as unilateral integration into the world of men, is not freedom.

Herbert Marcuse, who interpreted the women's movement in the early 1970s when it was in full force, observed that women want and need much more than a "repressive equality," a mere right of access to the "reality of men," with everything that this implies and demands as the denial of female experience. According to Marcuse,

> The fulfillment of the goals of the women's movement requires

a second stage when it would transcend the field in which it is now operating. In that phase, beyond equality, freedom would imply the building of a society ruled by a different reality principle, a society in which the present masculine-feminine dichotomy would be surpassed in social and interpersonal relations. Hence, the movement brings with it the project not only of new social institutions, but also of a change in consciousness, a transformation of the instinctive needs of men and women freed from the limitations of domination and exploitation.[22]

There is a trace of the radical insinuated in this passage insofar as equality, understood as submission to the hegemony of the masculine, finds its first rebuttal. Here, Marcuse captures the early signs of women in movement who were sometimes lost and sometimes found themselves advancing and retreating in their coming and going between the feminine and the masculine terrains. The price of unmasking a fake equilibrium which, fictitious or not, was ancient, would soon be discovered. Through the voice and actions of women, the unusual would be injected into the social debate.

By questioning the hierarchical division of the world, by affirming that the personal is political and that the political is grounded in everyday life as well as in personal feelings, by opposing the single model to be imitated with multiple projects and identities yet to be invented, these new social heroines were attacking the sacred principles of the established order. The collective expression of that questioning of norms/values and systems of organization came to be known as the feminist movement.

The Equality Trap ❈ CHAPTER 3

> *Oh, sisters, how we laughed!*
> *And today (as so many other times), I confess to you my bewilderment at the world, my fear, my rage, my ravenous hunger for everything. O my love that is unflagging but futile! Misunderstanding things and people . . .*
>
> *And in all sincerity I say to you: we shall go on alone, but we will feel less forsaken.*
> New Portuguese Letters[1]

❈ Women in Action: Feminizing the World

Utopias would be the most comfortable thing in the world if they weren't life threatening. Feminism is perhaps the most utopian of the "isms" of our time, the most disquieting, the happiest and the saddest of all future projects. An answer to the discord of an era, the one that hurts the most and in the most secret way, the least epic, but perhaps the most profoundly felt.

Two drowned bodies. Rosa Luxemburg was shot in the back by an enemy of her class; Virginia Woolf carried a load of stones in her pockets, which she herself selected. One body sank to the bottom of a canal in Berlin, the other in a stream in the garden of her own home. One died making history, the other inventing lives. Which of the two died the most?

Rosa, who wanted to be like a man, left letters of unrequited love addressed to the man she could never be. Virginia left a short note to her husband and best friend, asking forgiveness for the anguish that had ruined their life together, a life she had ceased to live. Thanks to literature, the androgyny of *Orlando* lives on; Virginia didn't. Fragile utopias of two women, renewed in today's generation. No fate is more foreseeable than that of a utopia, certain and sure of becoming disfigured with age. And yet, looking at it more carefully, feminism is young. Or, if it is not young, as researchers of the history of ideas and the aficionados of English literature know, it was swept up in an adolescent euphoria during the 1970s.

Twenty years later, doubts hover over the feminist movement, doubts that feminism itself acknowledges as perplexing. In the face of the derailment of a movement that would confront society, this perplexity is revealed above all in the way women interact with each other. Now, in the early '90s, there is much talk of ennui in the feminist movement. There are those who look with a certain nostalgia at their grandmother's portrait hanging on the wall, longing for a time when their plans for life, their dreams and future projects seemed clearer; for a time when the social, psychic, and affective space of men and women was clearly delimited. And yet, it was women themselves who repudiated their feminine cultural heritage, their stereotypical social roles, who took to the streets shouting for equality. Now, twenty years later, women are beginning to question their vital hope for equality as an attainable goal, their certainty that an increasing number of opportunities opening up for women would translate into equality.

The last two decades were the heroic years for a model generation that let nothing escape them. This generation had access to knowledge, to paid work, to participation in the social and political arenas. It was a generation that placed all those triumphs above the thin, ancestral layer of duties and responsibilities of the feminine world. They were Janus with one cheek turned toward the home and the other toward the street; they were women trying to be androgynous in an attempt to guarantee the continuation of the difference between man/woman that keeps the magnetic attraction alive. Theirs was an attempt to survive in a time of rupture with an age-old cultural code. That rupture, however, came at a price, a price which women are now paying.

The compartmentalized interaction of the bow and the basket in which each sphere held on to its own identity, its own experience and symbols, ruptured in an asymmetrical fashion. Industrialization and urbanization transformed homemakers not only into teachers and nurses but also into miners, lawyers, and executives. Cinderella in a suit and tie or Puss-'n-Boots in blue overalls, in the name of modernity and equality. That the promise of equality was transformed into sameness, or better yet into a caricature, should have come as no surprise. For it was born misshapen, unfocused, and it was upon the foundation of a misunderstanding that a political strategy of assimilation was built.

In reality, the role of each social actor is played out through interactions with an "other" in a relationship of exchange and reciprocity. That interaction is determined by each person's ideas, expectations, and judgments concerning the attitudes and behavior of the other. According to the laws of social psychology, no social role can be represented alone, and the interactive and interdependent nature of social roles dictates that if one role changes so does the other which is dependent upon the former for self-definition. In contravention to those laws of social psychology, the feminine role changed but the masculine role was left fundamentally untouched.

Women crossed the borders into the world of men, eluding the feminine side of life. They confronted competition in the public sphere, secretly dragging their roots from the private sphere right along with them. It was an unfair competition for them, but one they took on courageously. Thus, they were attempting to live up to the new profile of woman that was emerging out of the agony of a paradigm. They were obeying a double, contradictory message: "In order to be respected, think, act, and work like a man; but to be loved, continue being a woman. Be a man and a woman."

The relationship between the sexes, which had always been based upon the fallacy of the inferiority of women, now came to be based upon the fallacy of equality. Both men and women were so convinced of male superiority that women's demand for equality was reduced to the mere questioning of the barriers obstructing their entrance into the public sphere. Starting with the fundamental devaluation of the female universe, women themselves nurtured this fallacy, accepting the view of an egalitarian world as one in which they would merely continue to be the same as they used to be, but adding to their lives experiences which, until then, had been traditionally masculine. Since society as a whole, as well as women themselves, attributed no social importance to what women did in their private life, it never occurred to women during the early years of feminism to place the private side of their existence on the opposite dish of the scale.

Thus, the notion of equality was crippled from the start, and relations between the sexes resulted in a strange mathematical formula: feminine plus masculine equals masculine. The result of that formula, equating the feminine with zero, is what led to a psychosocial identity crisis among women, which originally had been the yeast of feminism. The more women asserted themselves intellectually and professionally, the more visible the crisis became.

Integrated into the world of men, the feminists of the 1970s were highly qualified intellectuals who had been nursed in their youth on Simone de Beauvoir's *Memoirs of a Dutiful Daughter* and in their adulthood on *The Second Sex*. They were the heirs of the women's struggle for emancipation in the early twentieth century. As they echoed the egalitarian ideals of the Rosas and the Virginias, they also confronted the perplexing experience of speaking from within the world of men.

At the core of the immense flowering of ideas that feminism brought forth, from the most hackneyed pamphlets to a significant body of theory, one finds the traces of self-examination which, throughout the 1980s, transformed the demand for equality into an anguished search for signs of difference. These are the texts and documents of an existence between two time periods, between memory and desire.

> In recent years, we've been talking more and more about our grandmothers as a point of reference and as a touchstone of nostalgia. We are a generation that saw an ancient pact be broken, a pact that separated the destiny of men and women. And, moreover, we are a generation that coexists with our own grandmothers in the space of one lifetime. We are representatives of a time that has passed but one which we thought would be eternal. We sit with our grandmothers and hear stories about how women's lives have always been; and we perceive that they were closer to the Middle Ages than we are. In so few years we have traveled through centuries. A pill swallowed and history is transformed. And yet those are the grandmothers who educated us, and they remain within us as question and, at times, as nostalgia. They are still alive and

they tell us about a time when, if a woman doubted the happiness of marriage or maternity, she would forget about those doubts as quickly as she would have forgotten the desire to fly that we all feel at some point in our lives. They tell us that some women pushed their secret dreams too far and most of those women ended up in asylums. The others, the Bohemians, happy or unhappy, may have changed their own lives somewhat, but they didn't change the lives of all women. The norm was always that austere, unsmiling grandmother I see in the photo, standing behind my grandfather's chair.

What is happening to us women in our thirties, who look at that photograph and see in it a glimpse of the past and wonder: 'What do I have to do with all that? How much of that is alive within me and how much is gone forever?'

We live in a time of doubt. Women live in anguish and uncertainty in the cellar of militant action. Anguish over lost security, uncertainty in the face of a world yet to be invented, that begins with us, without a model or a point of reference, unless it's a negative one. Knowing now what we don't want to be, we stumble upon the future and grope around for a nonexistent wall in search of support for what we do want to become.[2]

Similar testimonies were generated in the "consciousness raising groups" that proliferated during the 1970s. It was there that the "politics of the personal" was best expressed, there that women initiated a debate among themselves that would take on a much more subversive nature than the ostensible challenge that they posed to society through their demands for equality. Centered around a variety of themes and events, almost always announced by word of mouth, these groups formed, developed, and disbanded in accordance with the participants' interests. They were not sustained or guaranteed by any institution. Rather, their creation, trajectory, and eventual disappearance were a function of each member's effort to keep the group alive. This institutional weakness or, more precisely, this intentional rejection of any institutionalization, was compensated by a strong desire that was linked strictly to the desire to be among one's peers. The groups favored the emergence of multiple forms of expression consisting of memories, regrets, hopes, and experiences which, up to that point, had been part of their private lives. The constellation of small groups became the backbone and the vector of the women's movement, and it was within those groups that feminist thought of the 1970s was generated.

Like any liberation movement, the feminist movement garbed itself in a dual existence as both a cultural fact and a factor of culture. A cultural fact insofar as it originated in the dis-ease and the crisis experienced by a small group of privileged women who, having crossed the border into the world of men, realized that they were not at ease, that the dis-ease of the traditional homemaker was replaced by another nameless dis-ease: an inability to adapt. This female intelligentsia refused integration and was forced to turn its gaze toward women as a collective, toward female existence in its totality. It was through the encounter of those women with the others—the representatives of traditional female values—that a collective divergence emerged, the bearer of a counterdiscourse on the female condition. The women's movement can also be considered a factor of culture insofar as women's true identity, yet to be constructed, will be born out of the conflict between an irreparably lost identity and the identity that had been rejected.

A generation of women exiled from the traditional feminine, and strangers in the world of men, took on the project of "feminizing the world." This was a much greater pretension than the mundane demands for equality which were attributed to feminism in the early years of agitation. A militant text, titled precisely "To Feminize the World," synthesizes that ambition:

> Where were the women in that civilization constructed by men? They were marginalized, domestic animals summoned to perform endlessly the same job over and over again: a homemaker-Sisyphus condemned to the immanence of her everyday life, destined to center the world in herself, within the limits of her own body. Her body, her only adventure, her vital center. Kept in anonymity, protected from the tumult of the world, women reproduced their destiny for centuries, the same destiny in diverse worlds. "Childish," "irresponsible," they were protected like children, wild just like children.
>
> "Irrational," they erupt into History today, bringing with them an ancestral legacy: the valorization of the sensual, intimacy with the unknown, intuition as a form of knowledge, the perceived as strong as the proven, sensitivity versus the rational, aesthetics as an ethics of the future.[3]

To feminize the world implies redefining a basic misunderstanding. The feminism of the 1960s was a vindication of equality understood as women's right to participate in public life on an equal footing with men. It was up to women, to certain women—the most "able," the most "competent"—to blaze the trail in those arenas. These were the women who tried to convince men that being female was not an insurmountable disadvantage, that in spite of being women, they could meet the expectations of the workplace and public life. Little by little, however, women began to realize that their unilateral and exclusive right of access to masculine roles could only be explained through the internalization of an acute inferiority complex. Only the perception that the feminine universe is without value and, we might even say socially nonexistent; only the perception of oneself as belonging to the subaltern pole of a hierarchical relationship in which the masculine represents the paradigm to be imitated and the feminine the unfinished component; only all this explains the trap in which women were held captive.

Women wanted to test themselves in the masculine world, universally accepted as the standard for humanity, without asking for reciprocity. In doing so, they subscribed to the notion conveyed by the hegemonic masculine culture that their universe and lived experience were restricted and incomplete. Hence, it would make no sense to ask men to share them. The consequences of that self-devaluation were felt most profoundly by those women who had most successfully integrated themselves into the masculine world. The first victims of the equality trap were the intellectuals who had careers and who came to experience the conflictive coexistence, in each woman, of the logic of the public versus the private as a problem.

This matter had already been adumbrated by feminists themselves who had analyzed the proposal of the "double shift" imposed on women who entered the workplace. However, until then the question had been formulated in terms of the organization of one's time and the difficulty of reconciling one's physical presence in the home and in the workplace. "To Feminize the World" addresses the theme in its psychic dimension. An exchange of letters between two friends illustrates this split identity, the dis-ease resulting from that split, as well as the effort to understand its causes:

DEAR FRIEND,
Do you think we'll ever reach the point of being really free? Where do those heavy, unbreakable chains come from?

I would like to have written this letter to my mother. Naturally, it couldn't be the same letter, which is a shame. We should be able to write letters to our mothers. There are still so many barriers to overcome before we reach that point. Yet, we're certainly on the right track. We women are already on the way, despite the false impression that we're taking the whole world along with us. Can you imagine if the whole world wanted to follow in our footsteps?

Sometimes I question my courage and doubt my strength. There are so many demands. And, above all, there are so many demands that we make of ourselves, demands that are often contradictory, irreconcilable, and shattering, because they all happen at the same time.

How can each of us reconcile within herself the need for love, affection, warmth, and protection with the need for autonomy and independence, without which we will never be truly free? How can we reconcile the concrete demands of our children, who live enclosed within our family structures and totally dependent upon us, with our own individual needs?

We complain about the lack of time we have for ourselves. About the lack of time to find ourselves, to grow, to educate ourselves, and build our women's world. And let's not forget the amount of time and psychological effort necessary for the most important task, that of educating the world around us. Our most difficult and serious task is to have to control, at the same time that we encourage it, the disorder we create around us. Women have always been stable, secure, the most conciliatory. Suddenly, we've become agents of total destabilization. We're the ones who disorganized that supposedly perfect and efficient order, that familiar, tranquil, sleepy order. But that's exactly where I differ from my mother: that I should want a better education than what I received when I was young is fair, after all times have changed. That I should want to work, to assert my own personality, fine. It's high time that women acquire a bit more financial independence. But the fact that I should question my marriage—no matter how unhappy my mother's was—that I should demand my own sexual freedom which might, in the long run, disrupt my family, brings on exclamations such as: "But think of the poor children!"

Yes, mother, I do think about my children. Maybe even too much. I can't free myself from them, just as you couldn't free yourself from me.

What does it mean to be a mother? What does it mean to me to be a mother? Can you believe that, until very recently, I had never even posed this question? I, who have been a mother for so long . . . I had never asked that question before getting pregnant. I thought having children was perfectly "normal." And yet, I was not particularly interested in children as some of my friends were. Looking back on it, I think that bearing a child at that point in my life justified my existence. I hadn't been raised to "accomplish" anything in life, but simply to "be." To be a woman. And for me, at that moment, being a woman meant being a mother. It's amazing how careless and ignorant we were when we embarked on that adventure. But, sooner or later, for each of us the moment of truth arrives. For some women, this occurs when they realize they need to do something other than domestic work, when they finally understand that they are slaves to their children's schedules. For others, it's when they're finally alone, when the children are all gone, when all that is left to do is dust the furniture or wax the floor. Then they realize they had never had time to build their own lives.

I speak for myself. The school schedule, the meals, the shopping, clothes to be washed and mended; these are all practical problems for which we should find efficient solutions, my husband tells me.

But every time a meeting goes overtime or when I'm talking to you at the end of the workday, something which I love, why the hell do I suddenly feel that nagging worry come over me? As if an internal alarm clock were going off, reminding me that it's time. Sometimes it's my daughter's time. Today we must have an early dinner because she has a music class; or maybe I have to take her to the dentist; or perhaps I have to go buy her a leotard for her ballet class before Friday—"You promised, Mommy." At other times it's my son who is waiting for me at 5 o'clock. I promised to help him with his homework; he's already been reprimanded by the teacher four times in ten days, and, beyond that, I should already have gone to the school to speak to his adviser.

These are small problems, I know. All I'd have to do is be more organized. As I discuss that idyllic organization, I realize that men have a way of reducing almost all problems, big or small, to measurable, predictable entities.

For me, buying a leotard today or tomorrow simply can't be reduced to just going downtown to make a purchase that could be done any time, any way. It's much more than that. She and I have already discussed whether buying a new leotard is really necessary, especially since the old one was still in good condition.

True, it's a bit small.... Together, we came to the conclusion that it's extremely important in ballet for the body to be both free and beautiful.... The old leotard was already fading. So, off we went to make an "ordinary" purchase, it's true, but that gave us a chance to share an entire world of intimacy, a mutual awareness; we were accomplices in something and we invested the time necessary to achieve that.

Thus, these small everyday problems become, for us women, the affective sum total of our day. And we want to live to the fullest that affective life with our children, with our men, with the people around us. How can we reconcile that with our professional struggle, especially since as women we have to prove ourselves twice as capable, a struggle for which we are so unprepared? How can we experience this with men who think so differently, who aren't very sensitive and sometimes feel insecure about our demands for new kinds of relationships, about our appeals to their feelings, their tenderness, their sweetness, but with whom we want to make love in ways that make us completely happy?

We no longer want to be housekeeper-mothers who guarantee the care of their children, wife-servants who clean the house, worker-maids who carry out subaltern tasks. We would like things to be done differently, following our own rhythm. Caught every day between our own needs and those of the world of men, which are organized in an efficient and rational fashion, we rebel, we feel uncomfortable, we fight. We go off the track and the world derails around us, no longer works the way it should.

I have already told you how all of this weighs so heavily upon me, especially this feeling of guilt that gets to me now and then when . . . there are moments when I think that our mothers were right, that it would be easier if we just went along. Luckily, this is no longer possible, because you're there to stop me when I feel like giving up . . . [4]

The melancholy answer confirms the web of dissatisfactions and guilt in which all women are enmeshed; it is told from the point of view of a woman without children, one who chose not to have them in the name of greater freedom.

DEAR FRIEND,
This morning I woke up to find your letter under the door. I got up late because I didn't sleep well last night. To tell you the truth, I was thinking about so many things: about my life, my job and that everyday rat race that leaves us drained. So, I decided to give myself a nice, pleasant morning as a present, and I started reading your letter and thinking about you.

You ask me if we will ever be free. And you tell me about your life as a woman and mother. I was a bit ashamed, feeling somewhat privileged; I who can get up late, I who don't have children to take to school; I don't have to put up with children who come home hungry from school. The little contact I have with the "practical" side of motherhood comes through you, through your somewhat brusque good-byes in the middle of our conversations. The other side, that of an accomplice, of the pleasure we derive from a relationship with a child, that I don't know; I opted not to experience it when I decided not to have children.

You say something that's very important. You had your children without thinking too much about it, because it was normal, because it was your destiny as a woman, your way of BEING in the world; deep down inside you realize today that it was not a choice, but rather you allowed yourself to follow the only available role model, that of wife and mother.

You often told me how good you felt during your pregnancy, how happy you were when you gave birth. You spoke less about the anguish and difficulties you experienced in your interactions with the children. And it's only now that you're beginning to ask yourself what it means to be a mother. I feel a little out of place talking about this, but I'd like to be able to go back to the beginning, to the moment when we made our first choices, in other words, when we began having sex and took our first birth control pills. I would like to talk to you about those times and about myself, about how I experienced that trap which society calls a choice.

You followed your "feminine nature"; I rebelled. I knew perfectly well, since I was surrounded by women, that, from the minute children are born, what happens to you is normal: the home, child care, the constant worries, the impossibility of a job. I found my friends who had just given birth strangely aged. There they were, isolated, immersed not in their own routine but in their children's, totally alienated from the rest of the world and, I must confess, I didn't have much to talk to them about. I was a student with a passion for politics, and I really had very little to say to the women who were closest to me. I felt like something had broken and that they lived in a mysterious world where there must be pleasures that I was unable to understand and from which women without children were automatically excluded. Even so, I wasn't sorry. No matter what, children bothered me. No newspapers, no movies, my friends didn't live like I did. On the other hand, men always seemed well informed. They transmitted the sensation—and rightfully so—of living in the world, of acting, of belonging to reality, of being present. They gave me the feeling that they had a power of their own, and that attracted me. We could have a conversation. Some of them wanted to change the world as I did, God help me! It's just that they had the power to do it.

I soon realized that I too was excluded from their world because I too was a woman with all the limitations this implies. In the best case scenario, I was the exception to the rule, the indispensable exception that confirms it. All this came wrapped up in an undefined sensual atmosphere in which something was out of place: a woman; an object of sexual desire; but one who had in her something different, the desire to be recognized as an equal. A strange pretension, considering that we also want to be loved as women. It's funny, you know, but sometimes I got the impression that whatever it was that was different about me functioned as an aphrodisiac, almost as if men were thinking: let's see what happens to her self-assuredness in bed.

In spite of that, for the longest time I had a certain admiration for men, a sense of respect that naturally implied its opposite, that is, a certain disregard for women. From my

Manichaean point of view, men were the representatives of everything that lives, and to live implied fulfilling a destiny, which for me was, of necessity, of a political or intellectual order. To participate in that adventure, it was necessary to be accepted by men. So, I set out to do just that.

Objectively speaking, that was exactly what I needed to do because I wanted to keep my job at the paper; I had to be efficient and competent. I competed for that spot with men who were better educated than me, who had been prepared to play that role, whereas I was a usurper and would only have access to it if I could prove my ability to the point of exhaustion. I liked my job, and therefore I proved my ability. I passed the test and was called in for an interview. Then, when I showed up: "Are you married?" "Yes." "How long?" "Three months." "Within two months you'll be pregnant, and within one year you won't be able to work any longer. I'm not sure if it's worth investing in you, training you, and then have you quit on us." "But, please, I assure you, I don't want to have any children. I don't. I've already made up my mind."

At any rate, it had already been decided that, no matter what happens, whenever a woman wants a career, if she also wants to have children, she becomes a problem not worth investing in. I don't mean to imply that this trivial incident is decisive (how many of us have been through situations like this without giving up the battle?). However, it does show, in a way, the kind of hazards we face when we make our "decisions." But, as if that weren't enough, what did make me "choose" not to be a mother? All my decisions were somewhat intuitive. You know, just as much as I do, that we're not expected to ask profound questions. Why you and not me? You followed your destiny and I avoided mine because I wanted to do something else with my life. Yes, my dear, it's your fault if I ask myself at this point what I've done with my life. I can assure you that I knew what I wanted. To be independent, to be my own person. I wanted everything that was reserved for men. I wanted to make something of my life, shape it according to my own fancy, take destiny into my own hands without the strings with which you were blessed.

I became a free woman who earns a good enough living to enjoy the luxury of sleeping in after a rough night. What keeps me from sleeping well at night? I told you that I had been thinking about my life and all those things that make up our daily existence. . . . What happened to me? Why, if some day we're going to be free, was that particular morning so hard for me?

I have spent my entire life freeing myself from the forces that weigh so heavily on women. They are burdened with domestic responsibilities that I couldn't care less about. They don't have the training to compete in the work world, whereas I hold degrees that allow me to make a good living. So, what am I complaining about? Why, then, am I, like you, not living the way I want? You told me about yourself; now I'd like to tell you about myself. To speak at a meeting with male colleagues, you have to use the same tone and language they use. I learned to speak fluently that language which is so foreign to us women. But for some time I've been aware of a vague dissonant accent, a recollection of adolescence when I still knew how to laugh, utter silly absurdities, and act crazy.

I frequently hear people say that women have difficulty expressing themselves. I think their difficulty comes from not knowing the code which the world of men imposes. You get embarrassed when you speak in public. Not me; not anymore . . . I've been living and getting around in that world for a long time. Lately, however, I find myself growing pale sometimes; I feel a kind of vertigo, as if I'm going to scream: Enough already! Uff! That daily efficiency imposed upon us by a social comedy in which the dramas of the night before are now hidden behind the mask of a young, dynamic woman! Everything seems so simple at work: there one has to be brilliant, do a great job. There are times, at a meeting, when I feel like interrupting my own blah-blah-blah to say something like: Do you know that last night I was afraid I was going to die? But I say something else, instead; I continue to be brilliant and efficient above all else. In that game of prestige, I'm gambling my future, and in that game there's no room for anguishing over death.

Nor for anguishing over life, over that desire to live up to our maximum potential, to be a whole person. Exactly like you, I too experience that anguish to live my life to the fullest. I can no longer act out roles, no matter how noble they are. I, who always wanted to act, now, more than ever, I just want to be.

My public side . . . see what I've reduced myself to. See what we've all reduced ourselves to: a public side and a private side. To each of these sides there correspond certain demands and needs. You ask me how to reconcile these different demands that we place on ourselves? I simply don't know. But I'm sure there lurks in that question one of the most important issues of our time.

Ours is a strange society in which you and I, so different from one another, feel equally imprisoned. Neither you nor I can ever be whole. Something has been stolen from us, and as women we began to understand that. So, my friend, how are we to create a world in which we can feel good? I can understand how you get worn out at times. So do I. You know that better than anyone. The time when I knew all the answers to all the problems is long gone. (Do you remember how I used to be? I think I used to fascinate you, just as you fascinated me, simply because you were so different from me.)

Things have gotten so difficult and confused, and yet I still have no desire to have children, and I still reject the idea that being a mother is the only way to be a woman. There's a topic for reflection during your constant insomnia, during our perpetual vigilance. What the hell does it mean to be a woman? Perhaps you'll be able to tell me tomorrow when we go out to get an ice-cream at the lake.[5]

These two witnesses reveal a feeling of dissatisfaction, an emptiness that all women bear within them, the perception that nowhere, at no time, one is whole. It was this feeling of walking down the middle of the road, in an unstable, precarious equilibrium between two worlds, that led women to reexamine a paradoxical situation which they themselves helped to create. That happened when they insisted on access to masculine roles without demanding, in exchange, an equivalent and concomitant change—the access of men to feminine roles—which would have established, in point of fact, polyvalence for both sexes.

Any woman who has assumed responsibilities in the public sphere and has become familiar with so-called "masculine behavior" has been forced to confront this coexistence of opposites within herself. To feminize the world, seen as a reflection of a collective memory, depicts the experience of women who have tried to live out their professional lives without disturbing their family lives. Confused by the conflicts they have experienced, they discover feminine culture, a kind of historical heritage consisting of body and social practice, and they try to go on to an archeology of that culture in which all women participate to a greater or lesser degree.

Any job is a two-way street: the employee transforms the object, the job transforms the mentality of the employee, often without the worker even recognizing it. To be a mother during the long, hard years that separate the birth of a child from the moment in which society begins to take an interest in said child, requires an extremely active existence. The complete silence that has been woven around these decisive years is strange. In the final pages of Tolstoy's *War and Peace*, Natasha walks around carrying a dirty diaper in her hands and this represents, to a certain degree, the limits within which that aspect of life has been reflected in world literature. And yet everyone—writers, filmmakers, philosophers, psychologists—has been a child and owes his/her adult personality to the work carried out for years by their mothers or by another woman. The silence mentioned above is so complete that even women, in accord with the spirit of sacrifice inculcated in them, ignore that essential work which they carry out, or at least they forget it as soon as it's over. Ask any woman what she did while her children were young and she will answer "Nothing important. I just vegetated."

Try living from five to twenty years (depending upon the number of children and the space between them) being totally responsible for the life of another human being: their health, their safety, their intellect, their emotional and creative development, and even their sleep. I imagine that some artists and scientists who work on long-term projects may have some vague idea of what that represents; but even so, novels, symphonies, or particle accelerators don't get the measles, don't fall off their bicycles, don't wake up to the screams of a nightmare. Try living with a responsibility like that for years; don't you think you'd be transformed by it? Furthermore, if it is an entire gender that experiences this reality, how could their mentality be the same as that of the other gender which, when the work is done, no matter how grueling it was, has the right to sleep uninterrupted the sleep of the just? It is implicit that not all women are mothers, nor do all women take care of children.

Likewise, not all members of the working class work in factories. Meanwhile, in both cases, the collective experience is so strong that no member of the collective escapes the formative effects.[6]

To affirm the difference between men and women is nothing new. Sexism was based upon that difference in order to classify women not only as different from men but, above all, as inferior to them. That a text produced in the heat of the feminist movement should proudly affirm that difference—here was a change in perspective that was to mature slowly and replace women's earlier attempts to affirm equality. This is a prediction of a new concept of equality no longer based on similarity but on difference without hierarchy.

In that sense, one might say that the feminist movement has produced a radical, commonsense debate that has come about in two stages. In its first wave, beginning at the end of the nineteenth century, the debate focused on proving that women are not inferior to men and that they can do the same things men can. The second wave of feminism, which was sketched out during the 1970s and has become more clearly defined of late, suggests that although women are not inferior to men, they are also not equal to them. Far from being a disadvantage, this difference represents an enriching potential for the critique of culture.

By adopting this affirmative posture of new values, the feminist movement began to play what Serge Moscovici called the role of an "active minority." Active minorities are "deviant" groups that challenge "common sense." Through the firmness and viability of their positions, they are capable of provoking transformations of norms and social relations. In his book *Psychologie des minorités actives*, Moscovici studies the phenomena of "collective divergence" personified by "groups that were defined and defined themselves in a negative and pathological way vis-à-vis the dominant social code. They began to affirm themselves as groups maintaining their own social code and, in addition, were capable of proposing that code to others as a model or alternative."[7]

The feminist movement was the thread that allowed women to weave a new design into the social fabric. Their divergence is not a partial and passing dysfunction that needs correction, but a fundamental process within the existence of societies. It is the unexpected occurrence on which the growth and complexification of the social system rest. In reality, it is only through the deviant group's refusal to act in accordance with the dominant social code that allows changes in the prevalent norms and behavior to take place.

The first victory of the women's movement as an active minority consisted precisely in breaking the ideological consensus that involved the definition of the masculine and feminine. Masculine discourse had always defined what a "normal" woman was: her place, role, image, and identity. The dissidents of this model were expelled from the field of social visibility. According to Moscovici, "[t]he majority represents both the norm and what is considered acceptable reality, while the minority represents the exception, the abnormal, and a certain unreality."[8]

An ideology remains hegemonic as long as it does not need to be defended or explained. The effectiveness of its message will depend upon its capacity to generate a collective imaginary; internalized by everyone, that ideology is identified with the totality of the real. Nothing escapes it; everyone must act in accordance with it. Ideology can then remain invisible to the extent that it is endowed with all the characteristics of an objective truth, an absolute necessity dictated by the natural order of things. On the other hand, from the moment an ideology has to resort to arguments to defend itself, when it ceases to be perceived as common sense, its truth and strength are compromised. It is no longer the hegemonic discourse; it is merely one discourse among others.

When women questioned the pre-established roles and norms, when they penetrated previously forbidden spaces and produced a counterdiscourse, they brought two cultures and two views of the world into confrontation. Women in movement introduced uncertainty, plurality, and choice where previously there had been certainty, unanimity, and conformity.

> The minority assumes the psychology of a person or a group that is different and that desires to be different. It is capable of accepting disapproval and is insensitive to physical and psychological hostility as long as the tension continues. Instead of insisting on uniformity, which is the watchword of the majority, the deviant minority insists on individuality, emphasizing what divides more than what unifies. It transforms the negation of the norm or the traditional concept of reality into a new norm or a new concept of reality.

> Individuals and groups act according to the hypothesis that a person who is different from them is not a person. Only slowly do we begin to see that the not-I is another I. The intensification of the divergences is an indispensable condition to go from one social order and one point of view to another, from one truth to another.[9]

At the end of the 1980s, women began to defend equality, no longer in the name of their similarity to men, but above all in the name of their right to be different from them. The feminism of difference, which evolved out of the feminism of equality, introduced a more radical questioning and carries the promise of an "unprecedented and subversive socio-cultural contribution."[10]

The division of worlds into a masculine and a feminine sphere is beginning to disappear. Sexual dichotomy, understood as inequality, no longer appears to be part of the natural order of things. The entrance of women into the world of men tore away at the feminine. In its need for redefinition, the feminine, in controversy with itself and deprived of its internal coherence and consistency, now goes beyond its conflict with the masculine.

If the women who occupy the most diverse places in the world of men reject imitation and affirm what belongs to them as a way of being and a way of perceiving things in the world, then that experience will gradually transform them as well as the men with whom they live and work. To redefine the feminine is to do away with a nostalgic, already repudiated, past as well as the masculine model to which women tried to adhere. Reconstructing the feminine is the destiny of the women's movement. The presence of men in the world of women will also bring about the reconstruction of the masculine. Perhaps then we will be able to speak of equality, because true equality is the acceptance of difference without hierarchies. And the certainty of difference will remain with the body, and therein the site of greatest potential for a fertile encounter.

The feminist movement reminds us daily of the misencounters of men with women and of women with other women. And, it is for this very reason, because it touches upon what is most deeply rooted, most intimate, and most desired, that it reunites people and can therefore be called utopian. What if Rosa Luxemburg had shouted her need for love outside of her secret letters? What if Virginia Woolf had guessed how many women like her were grappling with the anguish of their inability to adapt to a mediocre, traditional concept of the feminine? That need and that anguish are the stones in the pockets of feminism. We must take them out quickly so they don't drown us, carefully so as not to hurt anyone. Show them without false modesty to those who live with us, transform them into a political agenda, break the silences.

The most hallucinatory of utopias is the hope of inaugurating within history, at long last, a friendly dialogue between men and women. Possible or desirable, that utopia is still unlived. Perhaps improbable. Whatever the destiny of the relationship between the sexes, the feminist movement will retain the historical merit of having denounced "the insatiable intolerance to alterity, the passion which nurtures our thought" and which "led us to see the nothingness in everything that doesn't reflect us, and describe difference as absence." The feminist movement will thus have made the feminine present and visible as body, history, culture, crisis, and political agenda.

The Coexistence of Opposites: The Logic of the Private/The Logic of the Public

The road that leads women from the demand for equality to the affirmation of their difference crosses into the "no man's land" of ambiguity, located half-way between the territory of the masculine and that of the feminine.

Women have lived immersed in total ambiguity for so long, the contradictions imposed upon them by society have come to coexist within them. They respond to the impossible choices by not choosing and they use up their personal energy in the exercise of ambiguity. Hence, for many women the result has been exhaustion, confusion, anguish, and frustration.

In popular language, we refer to the ambiguous as that which can be understood in several ways, to which several simultaneous meanings can be attributed. Clinical psychiatry defines an ambiguous person as someone whose behavior lends itself to different interpretations and consequently provokes doubt, uncertainty, and confusion. However, ambiguity is only perceptible by the one who observes it from the outside since, for the ambiguous person, there is no uncertainty or doubt; there is scarcely the ability to differentiate; there is a weakness in that person's capacity to discriminate and identify.

Despite the current assimilation of the two terms, ambiguity differs profoundly from ambivalence. Freud borrowed the psychoanalytic concept of ambivalence from Eugen Bleuler, who had coined it, and it was subsequently developed by Karl Abraham and Melanie Klein. Ambivalence serves to explain the simultaneous presence of antinomic and contradictory feelings or behavior in the same person. In ambivalence, affirmation and denial, yes and no, love and hate coexist in conflict, "the positive and negative components of the emotional attitude are simultaneously in evidence and inseparable, and where they constitute a non-dialectical opposition which the subject, saying 'yes' and 'no' at the same time, is incapable of transcending."[11]

The person who lives or expresses contradiction or conflict is ambivalent. The ambiguous person is unaware of what is happening to him. This person cannot identify or distinguish between contradictions that translate into attitudes or behaviors that appear together or alternately and coexist in the inner world and in the psyche without his feeling contradiction or conflict. According to Bleger, ambiguity is a "particular type of identity or organization of the 'I' that is characterized by the coexistence of multiple, nonintegrated nuclei which are able, consequently, to coexist and change without implying confusion or contradiction for the subject."[12]

This definition of ambiguity allows us to understand more fully the feelings of women who cross the border into the world of men: "The ambiguous personality shows the characteristic of not assuming the situation, of avoiding it, of not committing himself, or, moreover, of not assuming responsibility for the situation; its meaning, its motivations and consequences. The ambiguous personality is not, therefore, the result of a denial, but of a lack of discrimination in which nothing is totally affirmed or denied."[13] This personality type feels capable of shifting indefinitely between roles. When forced to make a precise choice, this person prefers to retreat and equivocate rather than confront the facts of concrete reality which would challenge his illusion of omnipotence.

In contrast to the situations analyzed by clinical psychiatry, ambiguity in many women is not a personal or an individual problem, it rather is an inevitable response, even a healthy and normal response, to the great variety of contradictory messages modern society hurls at them and which they must obey. In his study of the symptoms of schizophrenia, Gregory Bateson identifies the double-bind as a situation in which "the individual is caught in a situation in which the other person in the relationship is expressing two orders of message and one of these denies the other . . . [a]nd the individual is unable to comment on the messages being expressed to correct his discrimination of what order of message to respond to, i.e., he cannot make a metacommunicative statement."[14] A double-bind is a no-win situation. "Be a man but continue being a woman" constitutes a sufficiently serious double-bind from which women try to escape through ambiguity. The ambiguous person, inasmuch as he doesn't perceive himself as such, makes or tries to make conflicting forces coexist within himself, desires that are annulled or superimpose themselves without possible integration. This person shifts from one desire to another, from one existence to another, from one personality to another, in a desperate attempt not to lose anything, to be all things to all people at the same time. The ambiguous person is someone who does not admit a loss, who is incapable of mourning a lost desire: "In ambiguity, a person 'exists' but 'is' not; a person exists but has no experience; he exists 'in himself' and not 'for himself'."[15]

The fragmentation of the female personality creates a "kaleidoscope of personages," a characteristic of the ambiguous person described by Bleger, and earlier by Béranger. It is in such a kaleidoscope that feminine existence becomes multifaceted and is dissolved at the same time. Emergence from ambiguity presupposes discrimination of the terms of contradiction and integration of the "I" capable of enduring conflict. Since contradictions are not discernible, they work their ill effects unseen, preventing women from positioning themselves in relation to them.

The subterranean pull of ambiguity is identifiable in at least three examples of women's behavior in the male world: their equivocal relationship with knowledge; their painful relationship with language; and their fear of success.

Today, schools, universities, and research centers are filled with women who have not only acquired knowledge but produce it as well. However, even the existence of female-generated scientific research does not suffice to destroy women's mistaken ambiguous feelings of attraction and repulsion which act simultaneously upon them without one establishing its primacy over the other. The simultaneity of those feelings marks with the stamp of uncertainty an intellectual activity that affirms itself outwardly but does so at the price of an internal struggle to overcome the feeling of undue credit. Women's relationship to knowledge is surrounded by a climate of uncertainty in which two things come into play: the desire to conquer new horizons and, with equal intensity, a lack of self-confidence in, and frequently even discomfort about, their intimacy with knowledge. If self-confidence is earned through success of one's own intellectual production, which is sanctioned by academic degrees and publications, it is lost in the sneaking suspicion on the part of women that they are investing in something that is not worthwhile, as if some critical and, perhaps, ironic eye were viewing their intellectual activity as a distortion.

Considering that women belong to a culture in which their "actions and language alternate with and clarify each other, designing a field of representations and actions that are considered uniquely female, their incursion into the domain of knowledge—something previously reserved for males only—has not been with impunity."[16] The feminine realm organizes itself around its own knowledge—female knowledge is relational, founded in reciprocity, and realized through dialogue between two subjects—and accommodates itself with difficulty to technical knowledge that presupposes a subject/object relationship and that is carried out as a function of an objective that is allegedly independent of the subject. Female knowledge rests on experience; it is distrustful of theory which to women seems both seductive and untrustworthy. This lack of trust in the self is not theorized but lived in an obscure fashion, felt more than thought, experienced rather than affirmed.

Thus, contradictory desires coexist in women's behavior with regard to knowledge. This contradiction is not explicit for those women who experience it without formulating or perceiving it; they suffer its consequences not as a form of paralysis—this they have overcome and they have become involved in various fields of knowledge—but as a feeling of inadequacy, of vague dis-ease that distracts them from that aspect of their lives. This is what I call an "ambiguous/equivocal relationship."

A similar problem is women's painful relationship to language, women's language in the public sphere. Painful because dislocated or experienced as such; it is the language of the foreigner, of she who doesn't know the codes, who stutters, who feels uncomfortable and out of place. The thread of the discourse by which women justify their silence or, in the best of cases, their fear of speaking in public, follows a path of representations that takes its point of departure from a perception of public space as rigorous, demanding, and ruled by technical knowledge; it leads to the association of this knowledge with conceptual language and, ultimately, to its identification with the masculine. Thus, a chain of associations is formed which leads women to abdicate their right to self-expression in order to protect themselves from possible failure in relation to the expectations they themselves have constructed.

For women, speaking in public seems to signify a change in linguistic register in which informal communication from subject to subject, from ego to alter, inherent in the private sphere, gives way to another conceptual masculine register. This new register is experienced not only as different from but superior to feminine language and, hence, more adequate to the demands of the public sphere. The existence of two discourses, two styles, two forms of expression, one feminine, the other masculine, each a tributary belonging to a specific social and experiential sphere, was thought to merit close theoretical consideration, especially by feminist writers in the United States.

Among the empirical studies of female and male language that have been carried out since the mid-1970s, Robin Lakoff's research is of particular interest. In *Language and Woman's Place*, considered controversial by sociolinguists due to its approach, but groundbreaking by feminists because of its conclusions, Lakoff posits: "Language uses us as much as we use language. As much as our choice of forms of expression is guided by the thoughts we want to express, to the same extent the way we feel about the things in the real world governs the way we express ourselves about these things."[17]

Lakoff uses this premise as a point of departure for her analysis of the extent to which the ways language, as taught to women, as well as of the ways language makes reference to women, express and reinforce "linguistic discrimination": "[C]ertain lexical items mean one thing applied to men, another to women, a difference that cannot be predicted except with reference to the different roles the sexes play in society."[18]

Based on numerous examples taken from American English, Lakoff concludes that a "female language" does exist. It is produced by the socialization process and characterized by differences in its lexical register as well as in its syntactic-stylistic and phonemic structure. Compared to male discourse, female speech uses more adjectives, is more polite and genteel, and prefers modal constructions that express a triviality of content as well as an uncertain, diffident, insecure attitude. Female language also displays a considerable concern with purism and grammatical hypercorrection which tries to compensate for an insecure manner of speech. Lakoff believes that female speech, with its frivolous and futile content, its emphasis on emotions, its nervous tone and more irregular flow, is denigrated by male discourse. The latter is perceived as stronger, more affirmative, constructed so as to consolidate men's position of power in the public sphere. Since this superficial, confusing female discourse prevents women from breaking through their inferior social status, Lakoff traces their acquisition of "stronger" forms of expression which, until now, have been reserved for men. This claim has been strongly contested by the majority of researchers in this area who, although they agree that language and sexual domination are related, reject the notion that masculine discourse constitutes the norm and standard before which women should bow.

Nancy Henley explores a parallel research track, focusing on the relationship between "power, gender, and non-verbal communication." She examines the little occurrences and interactions of everyday life that appear to have no deeper meaning—for example, the manner in which men and women occupy space, look each other in the eyes, touch each other, smile, take the initiative in starting a conversation, change the subject, or interrupt one another. These are all "micro-political acts" that reveal and, at the same time, reinforce the structures of power and interpersonal relationships of domination.[19] Henley's research leads her to conclude that in mixed situations men tend to speak more than women and interrupt more frequently. They also look women straight in the eyes, touch them, and generally adopt a more relaxed bodily posture. However, women respond differently: they tend to look away or lower their eyes, to stop speaking when interrupted, and to submit to masculine gestures such as touch and smile. Each of these little incidents of daily interaction becomes a significant and symbolic gesture of the reaffirmation of the dominant male status.

The codes of gesture, imitation, and body posture are linked to the linguistic code in an interaction that brings into play not only the linguistic registers appropriate to each gender, but also the relationship of each gender to language as well as to verbal activity as a mode of expression.[20] Men and women adopt different linguistic registers inasmuch as each gender has specific areas of interest which influence the development of their distinct linguistic competencies. This interpenetration of the form and content of discourse reflects, on a linguistic level, broader social interaction between language, thought, and spheres of activity. Men, who control the use of language in the public sphere also dominate the technical, political, and intellectual register. Women command only linguistic registers related to things considered secondary or socially insignificant. While female speech is appropriate to the private sphere, it becomes hesitant and unsure in anything involving public connotation.

The diverse sociolinguistic studies cited above link the demarcation of social roles according to gender to the specificity of linguistic registers. They all conclude that a change in these social roles would attenuate the difference in language between men and women. As women enter the same careers and receive the same training as men, the uniformity of their lifestyles would erase these linguistic differences. Characteristic modes of female speech would disappear, one gender would become the other, the universal would absorb the particular, the "one" suffocating the "different" one.

This conclusion, however, appears mistaken since it does not take into account the fact that women's access to education and male careers is occurring concomitantly with the preservation of traditional feminine roles. Hence, we cannot speak of uniformity. This may explain why women hesitate, quibble, complain, and feel distressed. This integration, which occurs through the appropriation of the masculine word, coexists side by side with a "tradition" of female speech, a coexistence that is experienced by women as confusion and uncertainty.

In reality, the progressive process toward uniformity in the masculine and feminine lifestyles is incomplete and unequal. Women penetrate the world of men but this movement occurs without counterpart and without reciprocity. Although society accepts and, sometimes, even demands that a woman know how to speak like a man, the opposite is not true. A man who adopts a "feminine" form of speech is considered deviant. This double standard reaffirms the primacy of masculine discourse as the only acceptable norm and encloses women in a paradox.

Women learn to speak in a way that is appropriate to their gender under threat of being branded as "masculinized." However, to affirm their autonomy and independence in the public sphere, women need to internalize the norm of the masculine discourse. Once again the mixed message crops up: to speak the language of men skillfully will endanger your femininity. To speak it badly is to expose yourself to professional ridicule.

Women's painful relationship with language, together with their ambiguous relationship with knowledge, is a manifestation of an imprecise or poorly formulated desire not to give up completely certain characteristics of feminine culture that remain alive and dynamic in women. Notwithstanding, this presence still represents a complication for new experiences, life situations, and challenges that they themselves desire and defend. The control of the word and knowledge are, in fact, fundamental prerequisites for a successful crossing into the public sphere. For women, this success is both desired and feared; sought after and subverted; it is at one and the same time a seductive image and a dark ghost.

The third component of the problematic role women must play in the world of men is the fear of success masked as fear of failure. A game of yes and no begins: desires for change and ambitions in public life interact with fear of failure, with an incapacity to accept the challenge of their own desires. Women want to change their lives but they fear the consequences of change. They are afraid to question their traditional self-image without any certainty of finding another, more satisfactory, image by means of their entrance into the work world. They fear not being able to carry out their role as the emotional and affective foundation of the family without being sure of finding compensation in their professional activities.

Dissatisfaction, ambition, desire for independence and autonomy are feelings that are often accompanied by the ghost of guilt, and it is this guilt that failure sanctions. Since guilt is a feeling that feeds on proof that one is wrong, the best such proof is failure. The place of transgression, the public sphere, also becomes the place of atonement. Success is more risky than failure for women. Since success isn't expected, it carries with it the element of the unknown. To blend professional success with affective and family harmony seems to many women to represent the threat of a misencounter which they would prefer to avoid.

Already in 1949, Margaret Mead sounded the alarm: "The more successful a man is in his work, the more certain everyone is that he will be a good husband; the more successful a woman is, the more people suspect that maybe she won't be a very successful wife." Twenty years later, Matina Horner based her work on studies that deal with the representations and expectations of each gender in relation to masculine and feminine roles, and confirmed that one of the determining causes of the lack of women's professional success is attributable to their apprehension that success may compromise their femininity and place them in danger.[21]

Feminality and success are like two poles that attract and repel each other. This explains the risks of success by which women are guided: to avoid the roles in which success is possible; to do whatever is necessary to subvert success; or, to concentrate on "feminine careers" wherein success does not cause the same problems as it does when achieved in "masculine careers." The fear of success becomes a permanent feature of the female personality. If feminine identity depends fundamentally upon the approval of men, and if men feel threatened in their masculinity by competent women, a competent woman runs the risk of not being accepted and loved.

Judith Bardwick introduces another dimension of this problem. The anguish women feel comes from the fact that their behavior seems deviant in their own eyes: "'Deviance' refers to being or behaving in ways which are significantly different from expectations based on the sex norms and the gender stereotypes. . . . [W]omen's fear of success may not be a psychological trait, but an expectation that, if they come close to the male stereotype, they will be deviant and punished for it."[22]

Written at the end of the 1970s, Bardwick's conclusion reflects the optimism of the time: the massive, increasing entrance of women into the public sphere would be sufficient to do away with any notion of divergence and guilt. As Bardwick observes: "When we shift the explanation of the fear of success from a stable internal trait to a consequence of being deviant, we have changed the explanation from an internal variable, which is assumed to be permanent and enormously difficult to change, to external reality, which is easier to alter."[23]

At the beginning of the 1980s, a work without any scientific pretense enjoyed an impressive reception among the feminine reading public of industrialized nations. Describing in journalistic style what academic research had already established about fear of success, Colette Dowling confirms that the very idea of success takes on a different meaning for each gender:

> Women don't seem to go after success the way men do. They hedge their bets. They feel just as *anxious* when things go well as they do when rejection or failure seems imminent. Doing well—getting really good at something, *succeeding*—seems to scare the hell out of an awful lot of women who have what it takes to produce something substantial during the course of their lives.[24]

According to Dowling, the more talented women are, the more they will torment themselves about the risks of success. On the other hand, success can reinforce a man's self-image as an autonomous, independent, aggressive, and enterprising individual. For women, success is a source of tension and uncertainty. Successful women become immersed in a world of unknown rules that aggravate the difficulties of organizing their daily life and, even more important, risk compromising what, in their eyes, is the most precious investment of all: their affective relationships. Personal ambition, the creative impulse, the desire to be successful in the public space are perceived as direct threats to the definition of feminality based on notions of self-sacrifice, dedication to others, dependence and vulnerability. According to Dowling:

It's not that women court failure; they avoid success.... For the individual woman, avoiding success may not be as blatantly self-destructive as seeking failure, but the effect of this phenomenon on women in general can't be underestimated. *This tendency that we have to scale ourselves down, to step back from our natural abilities rather than risk the loss of love, is a consequence of what I have referred to earlier as Gender Panic—the new confusion about our feminine identity. Rather than experience the anxiety of doing (and possibly feeling unfeminine as a result), we don't do.*[25]

Hence, for all these writers fear of success is an escape from and a defense against the risks of fragmentation of female identity. And, yet, this fear—or its opposite, the attachment to failure as a self-fulfilling prophecy—no longer offers women a perfect alibi. The strategies of avoidance and self-disqualification both cohabit in the female psyche with feelings of equal and opposite force, like the desire for change and the need for self-affirmation. The poles of this contradictory interaction do not cancel each other out in a fictitious equilibrium, but they coexist in an unstable and changing manner during the border-crossing process, sometimes provoking self-confidence and euphoria, and, at other times, anxiety and depression. As in their relationship toward knowledge and speaking in public, women's attitude toward success is marked by neither affirmation nor pure and simple denial, but by ambiguity.

The feminine cannot be the location of an impossible synthesis. Its reconstruction crosses over into recognition and the elaboration of an impasse. For women to move beyond this impasse requires, first and foremost, admitting that they are engaging in a card game in which the deck is stacked. The winner is the loser, the loser is the winner. Women's response to these paradoxes and impossible choices could not be anything but ambiguity right from the beginning. The transformation of women's social status cannot be a change that will come about only in them and thanks to them due to their accumulation of social functions and, consequently, of psychic registers. Women's anguish coincides, in my view, with the beginning of a lucid reaction to a situation of ambiguity vis-à-vis a project that is impossible because it is badly formulated. It coincides with their entrance into ambivalence. For women, going from ambiguity to ambivalence means seeing more clearly, which is not the same as seeing more easily or more contentedly.[26] The women's movement today is like a mirror—a fortuitous mirror—in which feminine ambiguity is reflected. Yet, along with the passive role of receiving the image, this mirror must reflect this image as well. The mirror must allow the woman who contemplates herself in its reflection to recognize her fragmented face—which is constructed and reconstructed out of those same fragments—so remarkably rediscovered and which holds its enigma and its challenge. Only that mirror can make visible to the one who lives it the ambiguity which is inscribed in the facts and transcribed in the feminine psyche. This will bring about the transformation of ambiguity into a supposed ambivalence that is the conscience of the contradiction, of the yes and the no, of the tension that results from that yes and no, of the paralysis that resides in them. The image reflected back is of someone desperately trying to balance the desires that are canceled out and superimposed upon each other with no hope of cohesion—someone who goes from one desire to another, from one existence to another, from one personality to another, in a futile attempt to be everything at the same time.

A mirror of ambiguity, the feminist movement is passing through ambivalence, a sine-qua-non condition for rethinking the concept of equality. Or, what is equivalent in my view, to externalize the anguish that each woman carries with her like a collective guilt, depositing it outside herself on the shoulders of society. The feminist movement is a century old, but, far from having run its course, it has entered the last decade of the millennium with a secure future. The future task of the movement will be to arouse the anguish of society by presenting it with the problems that, until now, women have tried to resolve on their own. Transforming the neurosis of women into a social neurosis is the therapeutic remedy to which women will have to resort.

The Emergence of the Feminine

CHAPTER 4

I n solving the problems of gender relations, society will design its own profile and redefine the destiny of both the feminine and the masculine. The solution will contain a dose of anguish strong enough to guarantee that anyone contemplating society's profile will have to acknowledge the seriousness of its distinguishing features.

There may be some who see feminism as a fad of the 1970s, associated either with maladjusted women or with the demands of a certain modernity. Either way, it is now considered an outdated movement, credited with producing only token changes which time will discard. This contingent perception of what has happened to women throughout the twentieth century is due to the social sciences' preference for a kind of journalistic taste for immediate results and for what, at any given moment, might become the source of sensational headlines. It is much more difficult to look for the historical roots of a social movement, and more painful still to try to decipher this development as a symptom, like a fever symptomatic of a profound organic change. Over the last thirty years, we have experienced the frantic momentum of interaction between the sexes. However, the process of organic transformation of that experience will extend on into the future with characteristics that are unimaginable today.

The eternal feminine of the poets, which enveloped women in a veil of ahistoricity, dissipated into uncertainty and agitation as it came face to face with modern times. The 1970s ushered in a feminism that, in its desire for equality, sought to escape its limitations by receding into the universal. That feminism collided with a confusion between the universal and the masculine. A unilateral notion of equality—in which the masculine, garbed in the universal, becomes the standard and the ideal—presents women with the paradox of being themselves and the other at the same time.

An entire generation of women—an exemplary generation that went through school, sat in universities, managed businesses, got themselves elected to parliaments—needed to evaluate critically their experiences in the world of men in order to draw up a tally-sheet of gains and losses. It was precisely in the northern countries where a more advanced social democracy offered women the swifter institutional support necessary for effecting those achievements. It was there where the first signs of internal crisis in the feminist movement appeared, the first manifestations of a new dissatisfaction, the first divergence indicating a new process of complexification.

If the demand for equality with men was, until the 1970s, a transgression, a challenge to the established order requiring the courage and resolution of an entire generation, it is that same generation—the one that harvested the fruits of this equality and at the same time paid its price—which today is beginning a new transgression. Women first transgressed against the order that gave the masculine the right to define the feminine as its opposite; then they transgressed against the order that authorized the masculine to define the feminine as its imitation. By contradicting that order, today's transgression enjoys the extreme originality of refusing to be a counterorder.

The women's movement has matured precisely through its understanding of the ambiguity that afflicts women in the course of their passage into the terrain of the masculine—that shadowy zone which this understanding will have to illuminate. The movement will be that much more mature if it resists the formulation of a prescription of the feminine and tolerates the experience of indefinition, of a disorder that, as mentioned, is paradoxically organizational. To live with disorder is certainly agonizing; the uneasiness it provokes may lead to the temptation to recreate models, which is an indirect way of simplifying a highly complex reality. The recourse to the dialectic, always at hand in situations of conflict, attempts to bring to bear unifying syntheses upon irreducibly different experiences. Among the possible simplifying reenactments of the relations between the sexes is the myth of the androgyne intruding onto the stage.

In a book significantly titled *Man/Woman: The One Is the Other*,[1] Elisabeth Badinter employs the myth of the androgyne to predict the elimination of gender differences through the proximity of experience of both genders and to announce the advent, or return, of the androgyne, that dual creature made up of the masculine and the feminine. According to Badinter, the signs heralding that collective androgyny were identifiable, primarily in the experiences of women who were supposedly adapting to a multiplicity of social roles and registers with no great problems:

> Confident of their femininity, they use and demonstrate their masculinity without hesitation. Finding no difficulty in alternating between masculine and feminine roles according to the periods of their lives or to the moments of the day, they do

not feel that their bisexuality is a threat to their feminine identity: on the contrary, they experience otherness as the condition of a richer and less predetermined life. On the whole, women seem satisfied with their new condition and accept the idea of being men's "twins."[2]

Citing the Platonic interpretation of the myth of the androgyne, symbol of perfect unity, Badinter predicts a possible androgyny in the future. Men and women would be approaching the erasure of differences thanks to their already visible and increasingly more active participation in the public sphere, and to the still embryonic but growing tendency of men to share the responsibilities of the family, which will bring them closer to the feminine experience. These observations confirm Badinter's confidence in the evolution of the legal framework and its capacity to mold society so that androgynous men and women will emerge from it. She implicitly endorses the notion that the differences between men and women reside in their social roles; at the same time, she expresses her conviction that the erasure of those differences will result in a superior stage of human relations.

From my point of view, the perception of social roles as the site where difference is constructed is only half the truth. Today, women who perform masculine roles do not become males as a result of those roles. They retain the experience of a female body that exposes them to life experiences that are not those of the male body; yet those experiences are no less constitutive or basic than their social experiences.

Women retain a psyche marked by the feminine which psychoanalysis has tried to decipher. It has been described at times as a "dark continent," as in Freudian psychoanalysis, at other times as absence, according to the Lacanians, or as the word searching for itself or trying to make itself understood. The perceptive ear of Luce Irigaray has taken in with fascination this language which is incomprehensible to the receiver of a theory constructed *in absentia*, to this "sex which is not one," to this sex which has been decreed nonexistent.[3] Nevertheless, body, psyche, and social status—subject to mutual interactions that continually nurture each other—are processing the transformations of the feminine in the bosom of "that great sculptor," time. For women themselves, however, it is difficult to think of the feminine in this way. Trained in the schools of thought of men, when they try to read their complex reality and disentangle the dramatic quality of the moment they are living, women resort to the use of theoretical primers that obscure rather than illuminate the shadowy zones in which they move.

Sociologists fear psychologists and vice-versa; both fear the biologists even more. Hence, body, psyche, and social status are interpreted in an exclusionary manner, each discipline defending itself, the highly limited field of its own theoretical framework, its respective explanations of that phenomenon of infinite complexity: the human being struggling with life and time.

The challenge of understanding what they are experiencing forces women to distance themselves from conceptual disciplinary frameworks and to articulate, without prejudice, the theoretical apparatus that would permit them to read a reality constituted by body, desire, and social roles. Life, being multidisciplinary, spills over the theoretical boundaries.

Far from being an expanding occupation of the private sphere by men—reciprocal and complementary to the already extensive occupation of the public sphere by women—the attempt to re-read a complex phenomenon is contrary, I believe, to what Badinter seems to predict and desire, and which has been constructed as a tendency in the organization of contemporary societies. While it is true that today, especially among young couples, there is greater sharing of child care, it is also true that the organization of society as a whole is not moving toward adopting policies that would permit men to dedicate more time to private life. Yet the pressure for women to dedicate more time to the public sphere is increasing.

The workplace is organized around full-time jobs. Part-time jobs are poorly paid and do not permit professional development. Aside from artists, who organize their time freely, or the traditionally feminine professions, such as primary school teaching which, because it is feminine, is already viewed as a part-time career, almost all other job opportunities require a full-time investment. However, when both men and women enter the realm of full-time employment, what is at risk is the progressive disappearance of private life.

What Badinter imagined as androgynous were men and women, all capable of supporting themselves as well as carrying out the nonwage-earning activities of life. What we are experiencing, and what threatens to become the norm, is the disappearance of unpaid labor that characterizes the private sphere and the emergence in its place of an institutional network responsible for aspects of family life that used to be the domain of women. Institutions, businesses, and the state seek to absorb and deal professionally with the most intimate human relations that constitute the privacy of individuals.

Until approximately twenty years ago, private life was understood to be that which went on in one place, in a well-delimited physical space, the home, inside of which a person, a woman, went about taking care of a family. This job included the rearing of children and, in many cases, caring for the elderly. The woman, in turn, was supported by the salary of another person, the man; his salary was earned in exchange for work performed in a space outside the home where his activities were valued and remunerated in accordance with economic criteria. Women's everyday lives were characterized by unpaid labor that benefited the family: the everyday lives of men by paid labor that benefited society. This boundary clearly delineated a private universe where women circulated and a public universe where men circulated.

The masculine and the feminine realms were different and unequal. The impulse that led women to justify their access to the male world took various forms. Certainly they sought economic independence, since their submission to men was implicit in their dependence on the resources men earned. They were also seeking access to other horizons, other experiences, interactions with others outside the family, to knowledge and to the power to participate in society's decisions. Finally, they sought to make and rethink their sexual choices as well as the right to control their own bodies.

The eruption of women onto the public sphere is at the root of the problems of contemporary private life. At first, women simply tried to pretend that the problem didn't exist. They tried to squeeze into the space of one day what previously had been two lives; at home they performed tasks essential to the preservation of the family and outside the home they did work that benefited society. Tired, fragmented, dissatisfied, they began to protest against what they called the "double shift." They began to denounce the invisibility that hovered over feminine work in the private sphere.

However, this indictment endorsed a male field of reference. To the extent that work was defined as a public activity that was solicited, valorized, and remunerated by others, feminists concentrated on making society recognize as work the routine daily tasks that go into maintaining a family. Thus, they sought to attribute value to those tasks. However, what confers value upon work is society's remuneration of that work; hence, they began to talk about a "domestic wage."

Feminist vocabulary became laden with expressions such as "reproduction of the labor force" to designate anything referring to child rearing. In an attempt to confer social respectability on their everyday domestic tasks, women tried to fit their everyday lives into a conceptual framework that was completely foreign to them. They appealed to the economic to legitimize the affective. Their defense of a domestic wage, which would remunerate the "invisible" work performed by women in the home, was founded on two principles: "This work to which women dedicate from four to eight hours per day, on the average, is different from all other work. On the one hand, it is obligatory and almost exclusively reserved for women; on the other hand, it is non-remunerated work. . . . In modern societies, there is no other example of such a massive work force that is uncompensated for its labor."[4]

Two French economists went to work in each other's homes as housekeepers and performed, in exchange for a salary, what each woman would have done free of charge in her own home. By doing this they demonstrated the value of the domestic workforce, a reality already well-known in third world countries where taking care of the home has become the responsibility of a "domestic wage earner."

This approach almost always caused discussions on domestic salaries to end on a pitiful note. When trying to imagine ways to implement a domestic salary, what was visualized was the pathetic image of a housewife transformed into a public servant accountable for the quality of her family's life. Econometric glasses were of little use when what was needed was a close look at human life. Little by little, women began to understand that perhaps the most important issue was not who was responsible for the private sphere but what this existential dimension consisted of, what was its importance and its meaning, and what were its chances for survival? In fact, the private sphere is organized around affective relations and obeys unwritten contracts of mutual support remunerated only through reciprocity. The terms of that contract are negotiated with a limited number of people who choose to share the daily lives and an interpersonal dialogue. Therefore, the private sphere is, above all else, the site of spontaneous interactions; the activities carried out there take on a different character from those designated as "work."

The attribution of a market value to the activities carried out in the private sphere leads to situations that are frequently absurd, such as those described by André Gorz:

> [E]quity and economic logic appear to demand that everything people do be evaluated according to its exchange value on the market: the night the mother spends at the bedside of her sick child should then be paid at night-nurse rates; the birthday cake Grandma baked charged at the price it would cost in a confectioner's; sexual relations paid for at the rate each of the partners might get at an Eros Centre, maternity at the price charged by the surrogate mother.[5]

Economists and sociologists tend to learn the function of individual activities and not the meaning they have for individuals. As Gorz observes further: "They inevitably posit the system as subject (this is the defining characteristic of instrumental thinking) and see the living, thinking subjects as the instruments it employs. Everything, then, seems useful to the system since, in fact, it is the totalization of everything that happens."[6]

However, if we posit the individual as a subject whose work is not deployed for the purpose of commodity exchange and who is, therefore, not subject to an accounting calculation, our perspective on work changes. For those who perform this kind of work, such as the painter, the writer, the missionary, "the activity itself, not its exchange value, is their primary goal."[7] Mothers do not nourish their children to reproduce the workforce (although by nursing them, they are, indirectly, reproducing it). It would be difficult to imagine a strike for better working conditions in that arena. Nevertheless, if the concern with valorizing domestic work is so great among sociologists and economists linked to the women's movement, this is due to the fact that in a market society the recognition of any activity goes through a process of public recognition of its value and the fixing of a price attributed to it.

It was a huge misunderstanding that led women to valorize the world and their lives on the basis of salary; in other words, by adopting the criterion of value that was in force in the male world as the only criterion possible. They would do better to try to convince men of the existential importance of private life for men and women alike, not so they would be remunerated but so they would not be denied social value.

When women submitted the unremunerated nature of the affective and family universe to the logic of the market, they were trying to make men aware, in the language of their world, that what women do and experience also has value. Perhaps the time had come to invert the logic of that reasoning and expose to society the richness of the female universe which has, until now, been concealed, not only because it was unpaid, but also because it was unspoken and even unrecognized by women themselves. Perhaps the time has come to give up trying to transform private life into a job and recognize it as a commodity so precious that it cannot be sold and has no market value.

Yet, if this commodity is so precious, there is no reason it should belong to women alone. To offer men the possibility of noncommodity activities of the kind that have molded women's trajectory in the world would mean, in and of itself, a considerable change in the justifications of feminism which, instead of struggling merely for changes in the social statutes of women, would propose changes for humanity. From the perspective of relations between the sexes, between the public and the private, the logic of commodity versus noncommodity activity, we would be discussing the very foundations of human relations and society.

The process of rethinking the fundamental concepts of a new approach to social organization must begin by not reducing the female universe to domestic tasks. The legacy of a poorly digested Marxism and the search for theoretical respectability during a time when Marxism still dominated the social sciences led currents of feminist thought to disastrous reductionisms. In women we were looking for the worker; hence, much time and energy were spent on poorly formulated discussions about the relationship between class and gender. Because of those prejudices, perhaps the most fascinating aspects of the feminine universe were left in the shadows.

In the theoretical essays and political platforms of feminist discourse—in other words, at the levels of knowledge and power—the search for analogies of the problems of women and those of the working class, or the focus on feminine life in its work dimension, obscured the richest aspects of feminality. These aspects began to emerge from the shadows and silence, gaining visibility, once women ceased to resort to analogies to make themselves heard and understood, once they began to articulate a truly autonomous discourse for the first time. The field of reference and the concepts changed. Moving in a universe of values, women dared to speak about feminine values, about their own, yet different, feminine culture; this constitutes the basis for a new proposal of parity/equality with men. How are we to identify and name those values? How are we to prevent them from being reduced to excessive sentimentality and the commonplace in order to set them in their proper context of a fundamental and dynamic force within the movement of societies? Language is insufficient when confronted with the challenge of expressing novelties and naming emerging realities. We improvise with words such as "interconnection," "alterity," and "transpersonality," words that express women's unique way of being in the world with one another and among others.

These values form the basis of difference. Women are different from men because other values are found at the center of their existence: the importance of interpersonal relationships; the attention to and care for others; the protection of life; the importance of intimacy and of the affective; the gratuitous nature of their social relations. In short, an identity derived from interaction with others. Women are more intuitive, sensitive, and empathetic than men. As we have seen earlier, women plunge into those terrible feelings of dividedness, doubt, and confusion on their journey into the public sphere. At that moment their way of being clashes with the demands for success in the world of men, a world characterized by aggression, competition, focus on self, and efficiency.

Because women are the way they are, their entrance into the masculine public sphere was fraught with multiple problems and difficulties. The material overload resulting from the "double shift" seemed to be the lesser problem with an easier practical solution. The fact is that neither society, nor even women themselves, judged women competent, apt, or capable of entering the public sphere. For a long time, well-intended specialists cited the deficiencies in women's upbringing, their lack of education as disadvantages imposed on them with regard to their equal access to education and employment. In order to reestablish true equality among unequals, there was discussion about and, in some places, implementation of a policy of affirmative action.

Programs of continuing education, professional retooling, recycling of personnel, and improvement of the workforce sought to correct in women everything that came from being a woman: particular worldviews; inappropriate attitudes; and insufficient knowledge of the language of the workplace. As we have seen, these engendered women's dubious relationship to knowledge, their painful deficiency in the use of language, and their fear of success disguised as the fear of failure. Subjected to a rapid process of improvement, women tried to transform, train, and qualify themselves, never criticizing what they found, silencing their dis-ease and confusing it with incompetence and inadequacy. Wanting to be there and, at the same time, not wanting to, or feeling incapable of being there. Wanting to become masculine and being imbued, at the same time, with their feminine values, they feared the isolation and solitude that would result from the masculinization required to compete with men. In short, as has already been observed, the price of women's unilateral and unreciprocated entrance into the world of men was ambiguity. In turn, experiencing that ambiguity was necessary so that, at least in the spirit of a small number of women, there might emerge the idea of a radical renegotiation of the terms of women's presence in the public and private sphere.

The feminism of equality raised the flag for women's access to education, employment, and politics. It defended the right to birth control and sexual freedom; and it fought against sexual violence and women's subaltern role. In varying degrees and rhythms, in different cultures, feminism gained an international audience. Women's social status and the visibility of women's issues changed radically in the space of one generation. Despite Barbara Ehrenreich's synthetic polemic slogan, "Sorry, sisters, but this is not the revolution," nobody can argue that the massive entrance of women into the masculine terrain did not produce *some* change. What is surprising and revealing, however, is how *small* that change has been up until now.

As I see it, the explanation of that limited transformation is due to the manner in which equality between the sexes was negotiated. Women demanded unconditional access to opportunities that society as a whole—and they themselves—considered superior to their traditional experiences. To the extent that access to the masculine world was women's desired objective, that men determined what had and did not have value, that masculine culture was a reflection of what was produced in the public sphere—it became clear that what was produced in the private sphere, as a way of being, as value and desire, could be neither recognized nor appreciated.

Despite the boldness of their militancy, an entire generation of women came humbly to the workplace in search of recognition. To this end, women tried to prove—to themselves as well as to others—that being a woman (depending on the woman) might not even be a disadvantage. We finally accepted the double shift of work and the overload of physical tasks, but we tripped on ambiguity, which signaled mixed messages of contradictory commands.

Along the paths of doubt, anguish, and dividedness, we return today to our starting point, but not to regret our boldness and do penance for our mistake. There is no turning back for women; that is not what we want, nor is it what modern society is suggesting. We return to our starting point in the sense that, just as we crossed into the world of men, just as we learned its norms and values, we are now in a better position to reevaluate *our* world, *our* values. We do so not to take refuge in them, but to rethink their contribution to a new approach to gender relations and, by extension, to a new profile for humanity.

This is all the more urgent since there now appears—perhaps for the first time in human history, at least for the more developed countries—a new, unsuspected threat on the horizon. The very survival of private life as an autonomous sphere of existence is at risk. Here we are talking about one more paradox in a long series of misunderstandings.

In response to the demands of women for legal and institutional changes which would facilitate their access to the public sphere, some Western European countries and private businesses have initiated institutional networks—child care, schools, canteens, and shelters for the elderly—that have begun to take responsibility for the domestic duties traditionally carried out by women. These changes, considered a realization of the conditions for equality, begin to reveal today a much more disquieting side. What if the extension of that institutional network were to produce not only women's liberation from their traditional tasks, but also the hollowing out of the very notion of private life, with bureaucratic arrangements replacing the family, specialists for noncommodity activities, rationality, and efficiency for intuition and empathy?

Who knows whether the persistence of the tendency to make public that which is private, with the absorption of the latter's tasks by institutions, will not accelerate the disappearance pure and simple of private life or, at the very least, its weakening, which in turn would corrode the soil in which feminine culture sinks its roots? Then Elisabeth Badinter's prediction would come true in what would be a particularly perverse way and one would truly be the other, but in a unilateral and impoverished sense: women would become more like men and we would see the gradual but inevitable erasure of the diversity of experiences that form the basis of gender difference. The narrowing of these differences would reinforce the uniformity of society. The feminine would survive as a mere vestige, an object of anthropological attention just as the last indigenous tribes survive today—mostly in third world countries, which are more resistant to the encroachment of modernity.

The utopia of "the one is the other" would be realized. But

it is good to remember that our generation also learned the very hard lesson that, in its normative delirium, every utopia is totalitarian. Furthermore, in the two greatest literary utopias of this century—George Orwell's *1984* and Aldous Huxley's *Brave New World*—the realization of a totalitarian utopia implied absolute control over private life and complete regulation of sexuality. If we wish to prevent such a futuristic scenario from becoming reality, a different proposition must be put forth, but this proposition cannot be in the form of a countermodel, a ready-made, prefabricated counterutopia.

To envision their future, women must make an epistemological break; they must aspire to an unfettered way of thinking that will benefit everyone, including men. Above and beyond all else, women must resist the tyranny of the concept of definition that leaves no room for the imprecisions of the real. To speak of "feminine terrain" is to refer to something uncertain, something that is impossible to circumscribe or prove. Perhaps such a terminological imprecision would help underline the flexibility of borders and the very search for new words to express that which is felt.

In this sense, to approach the terrain of the feminine would be to accept an invitation to an understanding by approximation, by insights, which perceive the presence but can not and will not appropriate what is perceived. Understanding through approximation—the ideal of the concept—is foreign to understanding through appropriation.

There is no way, nor any reason, to conceptualize the feminine, but there is a way perhaps to sense it, perceive it, intuit it. And to know that from it, from that fluid, fleeting universe, can flow a certain, secure enrichment of the human dialogue. Feminine culture will speak, for example, of improving interpersonal relations, of understanding better the mysteries of those relations, mysteries as dense as or denser than the mysteries of nature. It would speak of more reciprocity with nature, of transmuting the primordial relationship between women and nature into a new alliance.

The relational flows from feminine culture as its deepest knowledge. The so-called feminine intuition—relegated to an inferior sphere of knowledge, situated by rational thought somewhere between magic and a kind of animal instinct—is a way of apprehending the real that traverses channels even women themselves were never interested in exploring.

The person who best synthesized intuition as a form of knowledge was Clarice Lispector. She did this in one of her perceptive probes of unexplored depths. In the passage I have chosen as epigraph to this book, Lispector recalls that there are answers that live in the spirit awaiting questions. Even before identifying a question, there is an intuited answer that dwells within us and is formulated little by little. Question and answer, then, are presences of a problematic that the feminine spirit embraces in its totality, knowing, however, that there was an answer which gave birth to the question. Nearly all scientific discoveries have gone through this process, but such discoveries, not believing in themselves, sought to prove themselves. Once proven, a linear, rational, logical story is told, one in which intuition disappears as an anecdotal occurrence.

Attention to human relations, the link to nature, intuition as a form of knowledge, these are features of feminine culture that do not stand a chance in the public sphere, stifled as they are by the relations of men with their instruments, predators of nature, and their appeal to scientific reason as a way to name the mystery. Nevertheless, women know how much intuition is useful to them throughout their lives, how much empathy is essential for them as a form of knowledge in the care of life and others.

Women are different from men; if that difference has been

presented as the foundation and justification for inequality until now, it is up to women to break the cycle by reversing it. A revalorization of difference does not have to weaken the struggle for equality, but it must certainly redefine it. The project of difference is not a revalorization of women's private lives, rather, it is a revalorization undertaken by women for the benefit of society as a whole. In this sense, the project of difference is postfeminist, not because it rejects or contradicts the struggle for equality, but because it corrects its distortions, critiques it as an unfinished experience which demands to be radicalized. It is postfeminist because without feminism, its changes, its accomplishments, its impasses, its questionings would not have become visible on women's horizon.

More than anything, the project of difference recognizes the existence of the feminine universe, that it is the fruit of a body that has become a social and historical experience, a psyche that has become a culture. It is that culture which today—through the presence of women in the centers of knowledge and power—has, for the first time, the possibility of declaring itself as such, as well as the intention of making itself heard and of existing in the exercise of that same power.

Far from reinforcing stereotypes of women as fragile, incomplete, dependent beings, without a life of their own, incapable of freedom and autonomy, the project of difference affirms the constitutive values of feminine identity in order to justify its presence and its impact on all spheres and dimensions of social life. We cannot go back to the past and return women exclusively to the private realm to mourn their immoderate and failed incursion into territories that would never be theirs. Quite to the contrary, an opening to the future is made by revalorizing what belongs to women—their roots, their identity, their way of being and acting in the world—and by opposing diversity to the unchanging, plurality to singularity, the uncertain and the undetermined to the foreseeable and the expected.

As a factor of enrichment and complexification of the social texture, the project of difference represents the sap as well as the vein through which flows true, unprecedented, and subversive gender equality. Subversive because it challenges what has until recently been considered the unassailable masculine scale of values ruling public life; uncommon because until recently women believed that the price of power was the renunciation of their own values and their imitation of men.

It is often precisely at the moment of greatest danger that the necessary ruptures and possible alternatives emerge with greatest force. The logic of the market is triumphant and threatens to invade and corrode the smallest crevices of social life, including the most intimate intimacy of individuals, with its power of institutional regimentation and its standard of market remuneration. Clothed in modernity, invoking equality and freedom, this is the dominant vision in the Western world. Positioned against it on the world stage is only one other fundamentalism, one of an opposite sign: that of Islamic unity, in which the notions of religion, race, and nation blend to affirm a different order, but one that is certainly subaltern and oppressive for women.

In response to this collision of fundamentalisms, each one seeking, in its own way, to define the place and role of women, it is up to us women to come forward and to look at ourselves and society from a different point of view. A change in perspective can radically alter a landscape, just as a change in theory necessarily frames new objects. Aspects of the real, until then unspoken and invisible, are lifted from the shadows and presented as a problem. This is so true that Einstein used to say that theory finds only what it is looking for: what it doesn't seek, it doesn't recognize or see. Therefore, it is essential to change the point of view, revisit the theory, and explore new horizons.

Accepting the uncertainty and the indefinite inherent in moments of aperture and rupture, women must open up a broad range of discussions of the present and future form of gender relations as well as the impact of that form's design on the profile of society. As a contribution to that exploration of possible roads and pathways, the following two essays investigate the question of feminine culture from two privileged perspectives: in the literary realm where the feminine seeks to articulate itself; and in politics, the public space par excellence, where the feminine proposes different ways of being and doing.

The Scar of the Androgyne

A word of caution: Avoid the commonplace, the readiness of a militant discourse that simplifies and makes obvious things that for millennia have been complex and obscure. Relations between the masculine and the feminine, mutual definitions and mutual exclusions, attraction and repulsion have been the site of ecstasy, creation, and also of tragedy throughout human history. Marked encounter, inevitable misencounter, the masculine/feminine relationship bears the stamp of incompatibility. The scar of the androgyne has never healed.

If long ago we were one, when we were divided we never recovered unity in our embrace. Separate and alone, we roam the world with such deep resentment that even after we find each other again, the fit will no longer be perfect; not even our tenderness can recreate the single surface of that one, complete, satisfied body. Mythically or historically, the masculine and the feminine search in vain for the unity they lost. In the course of that search, wherever it may take them, they each leave traces of their own culture, even if the two cultures dilute, change, confront each other and are fused into what we consider to be one. The scar of the androgyne is the most distinctive on the skin of the world.

Day and night, sun and moon, order and disorder, power

and fertility, logic and the irrational permeate our mythical legends, expressing in symbolic language the opposite poles of that union so fraught with tension. The body and life of men and women are associated with different portions of reality and each patrols its borders and defines its horizons and reaffirms the principle of gender dichotomy.

The coming of women to cultural creation, to the universe of fiction, was a political crime. The laws of the city always presupposed a masculine cultural world and a feminine cultural world to maintain the balance of the world without ambiguity. Literature was a domain reserved for masculine culture. Artistic and literary creation, the élan of communication with the public—a gesture, word or image addressed to all the unknown, anonymous beings out there—a voice turned toward the world, could not, therefore, be a feminine voice. Unless it were as a transgression of a basic order which, separating the masculine and the feminine, attributes to each styles and modes of expression that are their own and cannot be appropriated by the other sex. The coming of women to literary creation forms part of an energy that for centuries has been gradually opening a breach in an age-old paradigm, that of the separation of worlds. It is the crossing of the borders of the world of men, an uneven crossing which, paradoxically, also reveals a new horizon: the terrain of the feminine. Several signs show that unevenness: visibility, equality, identity.

In 1928, at a lecture before young students at Giron College, Virginia Woolf ironically, yet realistically, established the minimal conditions for women to transgress the physical and psychic frontier of literary creation. These were "a room and an income of our own."[8] This succinct formula permeates Woolf's thought in the various forms that the demand for equality can assume. If writing is a transgression that can be punished at any moment, then a room of one's own becomes the spatial representation of the autonomy without which literary creation fades into the subterranean world of desire. This room represents a secret passageway to the adventures of the outside world; that room lies beyond the thin walls of the living room, beyond the cyclical repetition of routine gestures.

An income of one's own is tantamount to emancipation papers, the dowry of the female sex; no matter how wealthy or poor she is, it goes beyond poverty and wealth. Otherwise, what would have happened to Judith, the imaginary sister of Shakespeare to whom Virginia gave birth in order to depict the *via crucis* of a talented woman attracted to literary creation in Elizabethan England? Judith trips on life, on its impossibilities, its prejudices and, abandoned, she takes her own life. She is born and dies on Virginia Woolf's pages without ever having written anything. No, indeed, Shakespeare's time was no time for female-authored poetry. What social entity could have freed the female soul at the end of the sixteenth century? What other destiny could a woman born into Shakespeare's family have, a woman with the same inspiration as her brother, a woman who, like him, might have experienced the irresistible urge of creativity? What frontal resistance would she have faced, first from her family—but she fled her home—then from the world of men, into which a young, solitary woman does not enter without having the suspicion of prostitution weigh upon her? Surrender, marriage, renunciation, suicide: this was a fatal trajectory that went from a desire born before its time to a physical death, the prolongation of a premature death, of a premature desire. There are tragic desires that bloom before their time and are destined to perish unsatisfied. Suicide was the natural closure to a conflict in which artistic talent was denied fulfillment by the impossibility of expression and was consigned to a mediocre, unhappy fate to which this same talent refused to succumb. Judith didn't have a room of her own or her own income. Nor did she have any rights of her own-except that of taking her life.

A castle on the shores of Lake Geneva with several rooms of her own would have made all the difference. It would have been even better if Judith had had the comfortable income that Germaine Necker enjoyed at the end of the eighteenth century, and which allowed the unquestionable talent of Madame de Staël to thrive. Madame de Staël, who could have paraded her status as the daughter of Louis XVI's financier through the corridors of the castle at Coppet, preferred the emotional thrill of a public dispute with Jean-Jacques Rousseau over his *Confessions*. She hurled the most acerbic criticism at the revolutionary Rousseau, who only redeemed himself in her eyes with *La Nouvelle Héloïse*, in which he demonstrated infinite acuity for feminine passion—a subject of great interest to her. If Madame de Staël the essayist gained notoriety through her challenge to Rousseau, Madame de Staël the novelist did not need this notoriety to gain recognition for her *Corinne*.

The French Revolution, at the heart of which was the idea of human rights, created equality among men which, in an embryonic form, advanced women to citizenship. The eighteenth-century Enlightenment illuminated the nineteenth century and opened a new chapter in women's history. Yet this was a moment fraught with tension in which expectations of rights came face to face with hostile resistance in day-to-day lived experience.

Jane Austen felt secure behind creaking doors that signaled someone's arrival: the doors were the guardians of the secrecy in which she wrote *Pride and Prejudice*. Charlotte Brontë presented *Wuthering Heights* to a publisher, without her sister's knowledge, as a work written by a man. These anecdotes give testimony of a time when the feminine was taking its first steps in ambiguity. The goal of equality on the horizon, still out of reach, was translated into a fiction characterized by bitter nuances.

In some of the best novels of this period, female characters collide with the limits imposed on their sex as against prison walls. Jane Eyre climbing onto the roof of her home to contemplate the horizon is symbolic of the frustration that haunts early nineteenth-century English literature. Virginia Woolf was right to lament that this bitterness was sometimes strong enough to turn into recriminating, tearful anger. As Woolf states, this is the venom that devalues the works of female writers who, in spite of great talent, lose themselves in laments about the injustice of women's condition. These works were generated in a social climate wherein feminine demands for equality with men progressively crystallized into the right to vote and the right to paid labor. The working masses were already reaching this point, not of their own will or by choice, but out of dire necessity in face of an urban, industrial life that pressed upon them with the weight of modernity.

The desire for equality quickly found its ideology: feminism. From the beginning the feminist movement intended for women to live like men, as free as men, since this was perceived as maximum freedom. To live like men, to enjoy the world and public spaces, to reject the conditions that cloistered women and limited their freedom of movement to the domestic realm, in itself represented a blooming and flourishing of new skills, similar to the tempting adventure of tomorrow. The objective of the feminine became masculine. George Sand challenged Paris in male attire but found a discrete life in the countryside: there she embroidered on the frame, lulled by the piano of her friends Liszt and Chopin. Women did not have feminine parameters of an autonomous lifestyle and, as a result, imitation of a masculine lifestyle became their sole model for freedom.

The same held true for the literary field. Since writing was another act of boldness, the act of writing in the absence of precursors could only mean to adopt, to the best of one's ability, the style that most closely matched what until then had been prevalent in literature, that is, the literature of men. The nineteenth century left a strangely mixed legacy: a literature similar to the masculine literature of the time, but pierced by a very feminine bitterness, the unmistakable sign of fragmented female authors trying to write like men without leaving room for the woman who felt excluded.

The first critical reflection on this ambiguity can be found in *A Room of One's Own* in which Woolf herself seems at times to fall into ambiguity, sometimes affirming that nothing is more fatal to literature than to think of one's gender, other times lamenting that women writers of the nineteenth century were so concerned with imitating men. And yet, these two statements, seemingly contradictory, are really not so because they mean the same thing. Because women take gender into consideration (although they consider it an experience of victimization), they try to imitate men and thereby block the spontaneity that would otherwise flourish in their writing.

This victimization, which characterized the first one hundred and fifty years of feminism, had its roots in a profound feeling of inferiority. Women's internalization of this feeling functions like a classical model of domination in which those dominated protest against their domination, not in the name of the domination itself, but in the name of what they believe to be their capacity to become the other. This implicitly legitimates the existence of the other as the standard and the ideal.

At the turn of the nineteenth century, the feminist movement subscribed to a strange definition of equality. It demanded the right of women to participate in social and cultural life alongside men and tried to convince society that feminality was not an insuperable disadvantage. The feminine realm tilts toward the useless, toward the socially nonexistent, the uncomfortable. Women saw themselves as the subaltern pole of a hierarchical relationship in which the masculine was the paradigm to be emulated and the feminine the unfinished component. The trap was being set, and the feminists of the first half of the twentieth century fell right into it: in search of the universal, they found the masculine.

On the one hand, the generation of women born at the turn-of-the-century reached its maturity at a time when awareness of sexual discrimination was already present; on the other hand, this discrimination was strong enough to make the most secure among women avoid identifying with the female sex as a whole. Those with sufficient intellectual and material resources, and for whom this discrimination was a mere abstraction, acted as if it didn't even exist. However, these were exceptional cases which eluded the limitations that still weighed heavily on women as a whole at the beginning of the century.

Perhaps the best example of such an exception is Marguerite Yourcenar. Yourcenar's life took a very original path, in part because of the unusual circumstances of her upbringing, but above all, due to the choices she made, to the way in which she transformed those circumstances. Marguerite's mother died giving birth to her; her father was fifty years old, the age of a grandfather, when she was born. Marguerite never saw the inside of a school: she was taught by a series of private teachers, who were all versed in classical culture. This strange couple, made up of a girl without a mother and an aging father, traveled the world, entertaining themselves with reading the classics which, although not understood in all their complexity, fascinated the young girl who was seduced by history.

> He was very good but hardly a father. Just a gentleman somewhat older than I was—I wouldn't call him an old man because

I've never paid any attention to differences of age—with whom I used to walk for hours, talking about Greek philosophy or Shakespeare or sometimes about things he remembered or stories he'd heard from people still older than himself, which gave me the advantage of a memory extending back over nearly two generations prior to my own. He was a friend with whom I used to visit churches and digs or discuss horses and dogs, a man who late in life reminded me of an old vagabond sitting by the roadside with knife in hand, eating a sandwich.[9]

That old vagabond, however, was heir to a considerable fortune which guaranteed his daughter a life without having to occupy her time and spirit with concern for earning a living. The monthly income, which Woolf postulated as a necessity for a woman to become a writer, was guaranteed to Marguerite from the beginning. Just as she was guaranteed a most unusual childhood for a girl of her generation.

Thanks to her unique childhood, Yourcenar was able to escape convention and, in particular, the conventions that defined women. This led her to proclaim that being born female was never an inconvenience for her, that she never wanted to be a man, nor did she attribute different values to the two genders; she believed that both men and women were of equal value. Moreover, Yourcenar was always extremely careful not to allow herself to be influenced by any political cause and, in particular, not to get involved with feminism—which she considered not only radical but also a form of reverse sexism. It was almost as if the problems linked to gender relations had nothing to do with her, except at the most basic level in which the defense of women's rights is confused with the defense of human rights; for an unquestionable humanist like Yourcenar, this was of the utmost importance.

The French Academy broke a three-centuries-old tradition

when it selected Yourcenar as the first woman to receive a chair. In her inaugural address, she limited herself to the comment that French society was misogynistic enough to place woman on a pedestal but didn't have the courage to offer her a chair. With one quick ironic remark, Yourcenar dismissed a topic that she could have explored at length with political laments or recriminations. Ironically, that silence was broken as a result of the fame she achieved mainly from two novels: *Memoirs of Hadrian*, and *The Abyss*.[10] In both works, her feminine voice is garbed in a masculine persona that narrates the existential and philosophical encounter of two men with the decisive themes of love, sex, power, knowledge, and death.

Voluntarily exiled from her feminine experience, Yourcenar assails the possibility of universalization of experience, the same movement of decentralization that allowed Gustave Flaubert, for example, to create Madame Bovary. Yourcenar, who was also exiled from her time, reaffirms her desire to break down barriers and accepts the challenge of history—whether it be ancient history through the Emperor Hadrian, or Renaissance history through the character Zeno, a doctor and alchemist who maintains a relationship with knowledge and its risks as daring as the one Hadrian maintains with the risks of power. Yourcenar refuses limitations through a simultaneous extraordinary effort of reflection, and through the humility with which she allows herself to be easily inhabited or possessed by entities invoked in a kind of trance—a mystic experience by which the mind is emptied in order to accept the divine spirit that occupies it during the process of creation. This is how a Belgian woman living in the twentieth century came to know and speak about power and knowledge, territories of the masculine which she penetrated along the road of abandonment and possession.

Although Yourcenar was reluctant to establish what she called "particularism" and although she minimized the political implication of gender relations, her choice of a male character to discuss these topics is indicative, as she herself observed, of the fact that the universal human experience can only be reflected in a male destiny. Women's lives are too cloistered, too hidden; a female character would be able to narrate the complex philosophy subsumed in Hadrian's memoirs only with great difficulty. The world belongs to men, and only men are offered the challenge to appropriate it.[11]

The sensuality of Hadrian, who was an Andalusian prince, is a Mediterranean sensuality with a taste for bread and wine, olive oil and meat; a maritime sensuality of winds and tides, of successive ports and islands left behind as the empire grows. These are the islands that enchanted the author's youth and imbued her with a fascination for everything that is Greek and, for the first time, the dream of a definitive life erased the mirage on the horizon. An Andalusian, a Roman emperor, but a spiritual son of Athens, Hadrian travels the seas of his empire exploring the civilized world in search of a peace he believes possible and which would be the fruit of wisely exercised power. He also explores the Roman cultural world in which the legacy of a still ever-present Athens cuts like a knife buried in the body, hegemonic memory in the interrogation of the human.

This right to the world, to the pleasures and challenges of the world, whether derived from the brutality of war or the sweetness of landscapes silvered with olive leaves, is a masculine right that is confused with freedom. And if the truth be known, it's the freedom of movement that the slave does not enjoy. But neither did empresses enjoy the right of a free man, the adventure of the world.

Yourcenar chose a man, an emperor, to escape the limitations of women's lives, to escape that closed, restricted field where the majority of women live. "I don't know whether we would be able to find anywhere a female historical character that equals, perhaps not in grandeur (that is another subject), but in magnitude a masculine character of the same time period."[12] This explanation from her interviews with Patrick de Rosbo confirms an intention already expressed in *With Open Eyes*. The restricted, closed field of which Yourcenar speaks, that of domestic experience, does not allow for great adventures outside the arena of love. Of course, a Roman emperor is permitted experiences such as war, travels, struggles for power, but, curiously, having completed the whole trajectory of that masculine narration, Yourcenar, perhaps involuntarily, not only privileges the amorous experience but places it at the pinnacle of her philosophical-historical framework. Passion is just as important here as it is in other female-authored novels which didn't dare explore a universe any larger than the home and its environment. Feminine voice, male persona. A masculine persona signifies here a desire to appropriate the masculine experience in its most forbidden dimensions. The character Zeno in *The Abyss*, with whom the author admits a personal identification she always denied herself in relation to Hadrian, is a transgressor. He is attracted by the unlawful and, in particular, by the illicit nature of knowledge and science during a time when science and religion were in competition with each other to explain man and the world. Marguerite Yourcenar's can be seen as the prototype of feminine literature that coincides with the paradigm of equality, understood as access to the territories of the masculine, the paradigm of an era that will only begin to change in the 1970s.

The crossing into the territories of the masculine may have been necessary in order to glimpse the still virgin territories of the feminine. Without a distinguished past, which Yourcenar and others like Virginia Woolf and Gertrude Stein provided, it might have been more difficult for women who came to literature later to establish a new, less defensive relationship of greater abandonment with it, one without any imaginary interlocutor other than their own sensibility.

It is through this loss of modesty that the feminine begins to emerge as the face of something new in literature. Unprecedented and unfamiliar, the feminine is expressed as a crossing of itself, as passion, death, and resurrection. The passion according to Clarice Lispector, Marguerite Duras, G. H., or Anne-Marie Stretter. The crossing of the territories of the feminine, a dangerous and unexplored terrain. The female characters here carry out a crossing of themselves, stumbling on doubts, as if facing an unexplored continent, reintegrating their historical memory, writing themselves and inscribing themselves in what they write. A cockroach smashed on a door hinge can be a sudden leap into the divine. Marini characterizes this crossing in the following way: "First it is like a wait that is unaware of its origin and its name, then a throbbing beats out, little by little, the rhythm of a project as yet undefined but, for the realization of which, all the forces are mobilized with a deaf and blind obstinacy to everything else. Slips will occur. The convalescence of a woman in her hesitant steps."[13]

To reintegrate memory and experience by giving voice to what was previously silence is Marguerite Duras' greatest artistic accomplishment. In her writing, as in sculpture, the voids count just as much as the written word; the superfluous is eliminated through what is written, implying a rigorous choice of words capable of supporting the expression. Duras uses silence as the white background as used in calligraphy; the letter traced against that white background is as important as the background itself.

We have left the territories of the masculine behind. Here we are at the border of a "no man's land," which is the enigma and the allure of Clarice Lispector's work, the unknown, uncharted place from which emanates a voice filtered through sounds never heard before. Feminine voice, female persona. However, the feminine that Lispector and Duras begin to express is heard against the clamor of feminism. A new perspective was outlined in the 1980s, one in which the search for a female identity replaces the search for equality with men. This new outlook expressed primarily a desire to give voice to that identity, to make the feminine known as a cultural presence, which is suggested in the literature bearing the rubric "Writing the Body."

From the point of view of the sociology of literature, writing the body expresses the moment in which women sketch out an identity that is neither the flipside of male identity nor its opposite. A collective subject writes and inscribes itself on this body-author. In psychoanalytic terms, female identity ceases to be the "other of the same" in order to become a search and a creation. The era of the "second sex" was over, when Simone de Beauvoir proposed equality against fact and myth. Now it is a question of what Luce Irigaray calls "the sex which is not one," whose turn it is to create itself.

Literature will collaborate in this creation by employing the material body. From Plato to Freud, Irigaray outlines a scientific history that constructs the notion of woman both in the image of man and in his service. But her speculum reveals another woman, one who is not submissive to the logic of the masculine.[14] She traverses those texts in which the masculine determines the limits of the feminine as "other" and confirms the feminine as a negative alteration of the "same" as a necessary act for the "sex which is not one," which was never one, to become one by breaking the silence its exclusion from discourse had imposed.

Fiction and theory collaborate in the sense that they create a *tabula rasa* of the past. The inequality between men and women proceeds from that "defect," from that inferiority of a sex that could only be a deformation of the other. The struggle for equality tried to deny the existence of that defect in order to deny any difference whatsoever. But that same struggle ignored the fact that, by denying the defect, it was subscribing to the criterion of symmetry and was seeking recognition in the name of its capacity to be like the other, rather than in the name of being the other. This was the trap the vanguard of the 1970s rejected through its dislocation to another position from which it won a voice for women, a voice that authored an unknown discourse. Irigaray takes this position to an extreme as she poses questions such as: Since the female sex was censured from the standpoint of the laws of the conscious mind, does the feminine even have an unconscious? Wouldn't the feminine itself be the unconscious? Wouldn't the unconscious be that repressed feminine whose return is revealed through the pleasure of women Freud never knew how to listen to?

An era that legitimizes this type of theoretical boldness encourages autobiographical, cathartic, and associative discourse on the literary plane. Such discourse is understood as the unconscious and, like the unconscious, it ignores its justification, attributing to itself an intrinsic, self-referential, and self-decodifiable meaning. The seminal work of this literary trend is Annie Leclerc's *Parole de femme*. Published in France in 1974, it has enjoyed enormous success. An extraordinary praise of menstruation, childbirth, female pleasure, an amazing exercise of self-contemplation, *Parole de femme*, although credited with ignoring taboos, cannot be considered a literary work. It is poor in its formal structure and in its desire to recover the delights of feminality, which are obscured and disdained by masculine culture. This book pushes the author dangerously close to a reverse sexism which seems almost ridiculous outside the hothouse of militant feminism. But the fact remains, Paris in the 1970s was such a hothouse and, for that very reason, the book ushered in a period of increased production in which many women believed that testimonial literature, more autobiographical than fictional, would succeed in giving expression to the feminine, in revealing its unexplored richness. The harvest of this crop is most disappointing, however. The majority of the works published are testimonials that amount to not much more than uterine floods of interior pulsations and rhythms.

Convinced that the lack of female representation in the literary world is caused by the sexism of masculine hegemonic culture, the feminist movement encouraged women to write. But, in this encouragement, the movement confused the importance of the act of self-expression—more women writing more freely—with the importance of what was being stated. Few writers of this period achieved literary distinction; the majority simply took advantage of the revolutionary climate of the times.

Hélène Cixous, writer and philosopher of the project known as "Writing the Body," is one of the few exceptions. In her book *Coming to Writing*, Cixous synthesizes the ideology of the body as a metaphor:

> Life becomes text starting out from my body. I am already text. History, love, violence, time, work, desire inscribe it in my body, I go where the 'fundamental language' is spoken, the body language into which all the tongues of things, acts, and beings translate themselves, in my own breast, the whole of reality worked upon in my flesh, intercepted by my nerves, by my senses, by the labor of all my cells, projected, analyzed, recomposed into a book.[15]

Menstruation, childbirth, nursing, the breasts, the vagina, the uterus are not only the body itself but a metaphor of a perception of the world as experienced from the standpoint of that specific, irreplaceable dwelling of the feminine.

Cixous presents her novel *Souffles* as a meditation and a psalm about the passion of a woman crossing the great mythic bodies of Greece and Palestine where the masculine and the feminine are fused: "Blind and seeing, she traverses the young erotic spaces of bisexuality. Text-mother and text-child at one and the same time, text-love: space of genesis. Let the milk run! Let the writing flow!"[16]

There is a certain circularity that characterizes writing the body, that springs from it, which believes that pleasure is a form of knowledge, and which returns to pleasure as one returns to a safe port; the body is point of departure, journey, and arrival. Writing the body would be nothing more than a literary trend which may or may not please the reader; but it would have no theoretical significance if it did not bring with it the, indeed, more interesting debate over the existence of feminine writing. Does there exist, in fact, a feminine writing?

Two issues surrounding this debate have been misunderstood: Is there a feminine writing made up of identifiable themes and styles as well as female authors? Or is there a feminist writing that aspires to bring women's present-day search for social and sexual identity into the literary field?

The first question presupposes the existence of a feminine which, for sociocultural, historical, biological, or all three reasons, would reside in the writer herself. It would act on the writer, consciously or unconsciously, with deterministic power, and would become noticeable, perceptible, in the finished work. Beyond writing, this question opens up the debate over the existence of a feminine culture, an offshoot of the particularities of the body in which women's literature has its roots. This is a more precise and more comprehensive way of approaching difference than placing it on a purely libidinal plane. This supposed feminine culture should be understood here in an anthropological sense, in other words, as the expression of ways of acting and speaking that accompany the feminine experience that has been traditionally separated from the masculine experience.

The French ethnographer Yvonne Verdier established a direct relationship between the body, the behavior, and the language of women, thus corroborating the hypothesis of the existence of feminine culture:

> The same thread runs through the plot made up of phrases, gestures, and feminine roles, the philosophical thread of the particularities of her body. Ways of speaking and acting alternate and shed light on each other, mapping a sphere of representations and actions that belong characteristically to women. The feminine universe is not defined negatively in relation to the world of men, but from the inside out, in and of itself, as a universe organized and governed by its own laws, a woman's exclusive place of sovereignty and autonomy.[17]

With modernity came the approximation of worlds. Women became more and more visible in the territories of the masculine. The very act of writing is a symptom of that proximity. However, this is not sufficient to erase the underlying dichotomy that causes masculine and feminine, as body and existential experience, to recall the scar of the androgyne, the borderline marking the limitations that define the horizons of each. As we have already observed, this means that two cultures coexist, living together, but disguised as only one. A primordial feminine culture consisting of physical and psychic experience now turns up in feminine expression. Whether women express their bitterness against discrimination, write in support of equality or to underline difference, it is still identity that is being pursued along the paths of difference and diversity.

The presence of the feminine in literature can only be delimited as a crisis. It is the feminine in crisis, struggling with ambiguity and indefinition, that is manifested in literature—and not in a predetermined and therefore predictable feminine. The literary feminine is ambiguous and in search of itself, just like the women of our times; both the yes and the no, both equality and difference fit into the category of the feminine. These poles exist like isolated nuclei, just as in the everyday experience of women who sometimes live like men and sometimes like women, and between these two poles oscillates an identity in crisis.

Only literary history will be able to say whether at the end of the twentieth century a feminine literature that is contemporaneous with feminism will have appeared. Perhaps that critical distance will illuminate today's reality with a clarity that our proximity to the event tends to obscure. Our contemporary view is formed in a dark room, in which we try little by little to adapt our vision in order to discern contours and identify recognizable shapes. For that very reason, any conclusion at the moment is tentative.

In reaction to an attempt by critics to identify her personally with her characters, Marguerite Yourcenar illustrates the author's intimacy with her work without confusing author and work. According to Yourcenar, her characters feed on her like a child who, although suckled on mother's milk, is still a separate being. That metaphor of maternity, in which she affirms the filiation as well as the independence of the work, leads us to think that if feminine culture does exist, even involuntarily, like sap it will nourish the work of art, marking it with the stamp of the feminine.

In *Letters to a Young Poet*, the German poet Rilke refers to "our ancestors' blood" which "incessantly moves in us and combines with our own to form the unique, unrepeatable being that we are at every turning of our life."[18] He summarizes the difficult interplay between the individual and the collective, the present and the past, and the author and his/her culture which is so decisive in literary production. He defines the unique, indispensable character of the author as well as his fatal insertion in his own time.

In the women writing today we see the simultaneous existence of the mothers and grandmothers who concealed their diaries; the experience of the freedom of expression; and the ambiguity vis-à-vis one's own identity. In the women who are writing today there is a feminine tradition that, together with the experience of androgyny, is generating something completely new, something that will never happen again. Perhaps this is what we call the feminine in literature.

As far as the existence of a feminist writing is concerned, it is born of authors who, in harmony with the spirit of their times, try to imprint voluntarily on their texts impressions of the feminine which they would like to make indelible. Writing the body imposes itself like erotic and political desire. In "The Laugh of the Medusa," Hélène Cixous summarizes this position as something women must do: "Woman must write her self: must write about women and bring women to writing from which they have been driven away as violently as from their bodies—for the same reasons, by the same law, with the same fatal goal. Woman must put herself into the text—as into the world and into history—by her own movement."[19]

But perhaps the risk and the inevitability of all militancy is that of creating a norm outside of which women once more feel inadequate. The value of neofeminism, which denied at the same time a restrictive past and an acritical adhesion to the masculine universe as an option to that past, would have been that of opening up for women the possibility of multiplicity and the new. This would not have consisted of the superimposition of feminine and masculine experiences, but—depending on the spices chosen by each woman—of an infinite gamut of mixtures of those elements. In other words, freedom.

Feminist literature of the 1970s, or that which is called feminist, is analogous to "socialist realism" in the women's movement. To write with the body is at times confused with an infinite flow of milk and blood, thus alluding in an exaggerated way to the irreducibility of women's experiences, a kind of kitsch of difference now so widely accepted and proclaimed. Writing the body is only one of the ways, and not necessarily the most faithful or the most creative, of revealing the crisis of the feminine. Its value, just like that of all art deserving of the name, is to make the invisible visible; in this case the feminine libido which has been obscured by the self-referential masculine libido. Its danger is to try to keep that feminine within the borders of a style that reveals itself as polymorphous and inexhaustible.

As far as the emergence of the feminine in literature is concerned, it presupposes at least two conditions: the first is that women be free to write what they feel without mental interlocutors or phantasmagorical critics who, seated on their shoulders, correct the text and introduce background noises that should not exist. In an article titled "Professions for Women," Virginia Woolf proposed killing the angel of the hearth. The angel of the hearth was that receptive woman who preferred death to disappointing someone and who guaranteed the happiness of everyone except her own. Neofeminism has already felled that angel. However, there remains that insidious devil of feminism itself which spears with the trident of the command: "Write like a woman."

In a certain way, it is in the movement itself that female identity seeks and attempts to write itself. It is in the testimony to confusion, uncertainty, the hidden, the occult, the sensibility of the unknown that the feminine will yield up its territories so that a literature may flourish in them.

❋ The Logic of the Madwomen of the Plaza de Mayo

There is a square in Buenos Aires that must be visited by all the most determined tourists, those who have their pictures taken by the numerous old-fashioned cameras and return home with sepia-colored photos with the Cabildo or the Casa Rosada in the background. The Plaza de Mayo is the heart of the old city, the stage of Argentine history, the sounding board that murmurs with echoes of political coups and countercoups.[20] From the balconies of the Casa Rosada, the seat of political power, Evita promised the "shirtless ones," the so-called "orphaned" working class, the protection that she and her husband Juan Perón used to mobilize the forgotten impoverished classes of Argentina.

One day, many years later, a large group of women came on stage in the Plaza de Mayo. Their dramatic theme still had to do with orphans, but this time in reverse; the orphans were those mothers of the "disappeared" children, the children who had been lost in the sordid intrigues of the Argentine military dictatorship. In silence, head covered with white kerchiefs, each woman carried a sign with the name of her "disappeared" child. These women would break their silence only to shout out that name. The procession circled the Plaza de Mayo relentlessly, for days, months, and years, bearing on their shoulders the tragic weight of confronting the impossible; because they were asking for the impossible. They were asking for their children, dead certainly, but dead where? Killed by whom? Or were they perhaps still alive? If so, where were they?

The military dictatorship dubbed these modern-day Antigones "the madwomen of the Plaza de Mayo." They were common women, people just like us; not heroines, they were each one of us and our circumstances. Under an open sky these women challenged a bloodthirsty power which, tormented by paranoia, had pushed its most innocent victims into the shadows. There the women would come, day after day, rain or shine, in the full light of day, under the very windows of the dictator. Through their silence, pierced only by the shouted names, they made themselves heard like the chant of a litany that echoed throughout the country, throughout Latin America, and beyond the seas.

These women were creating the most important, most eloquent, and most clearly understood political event of our times. In silence. They were "mad," decreed the dictator, convinced of his own logic. "Mad," said the politicians of the opposition parties who criticized the women's intransigence, their refusal to enter into any pact, agreement, or negotiation. They were "mad," said the complacent Argentine Church, proclaiming that the time had come to forget the dead and take care of the living. But these women were unwilling to forget. They were "mad." They were the Madwomen of the Plaza de Mayo.

Within history, they were confronting the logic of history with another history. And in this way they were giving the lie to a curse weighing upon women who had always been accused of supporting the conservative in politics. This reputation grew out of a misunderstanding. It is true that modern history records the existence of women's organizations that were created as the mouthpieces of conservative ideas; hence, the assumption was immediately made that women were inherently conservative. But hasty interpretation ignores not only the causes but the deeper meaning of their supposed conservatism.

Women's fear of change is not necessarily an innate conservatism. It is their instinctive defense mechanism against decisions that, once made, may, much to their surprise, endanger their children, husbands, and other menfolk. Women's relationship to politics has traditionally been an experience of opposition. Locked in their homes, women created a life for themselves aside from the experience of seeing their homes transformed by external events, the logic of which escaped them. They were never consulted about these events which were not of their own choosing but which affected their lives like a bolt of lightning out of the blue, unexplained and, for that very reason, frightening. Politics contained an element of threat which they quickly transformed into a fear of change.

Women's ancestral relationship of powerlessness vis-à-vis politics is recorded in the museum at Delphi in fragments of a Roman frieze with sculptures depicting the struggle between men and the women who were trying to prevent them from going off to war. At the end of the succession of sculptures, the women are depicted as beaten off, defeated, fallen to the ground, left behind by a proud, powerful expedition heading for new conquests and victories. The Roman frieze is an allegory of an action repeated thousands of times by mothers and spouses, regardless of their political positions. Their conservatism does not necessarily imply their adherence to conservative political ideas, but a visceral distrust of politics as a Pandora's box.

Women's suffrage reinforced that conservative image insofar as women often vote against platforms of change. The left, which sees itself as the standard-bearer of social progress, has always feared the feminine vote which it considers reactionary. What happened was that the right to vote admitted women to a formal but not substantive citizenship. On a daily basis, most women still remain excluded from political life, linked in an umbilical fashion to their families and isolated from information. This results in their presence in the polis, a presence exercised through the vote but coexisting with a resistance to change which is expressed in the content of their vote.

However, politics lives not by votes alone, and elections are not the only measure of the quality of female participation in the polis. Women can suddenly be set into action for other reasons and, at the service of the deeper meaning of those reasons, can emerge politically with new content. There is pain that is redemptive: "But when you no longer wait/For the tide,/ Here is the knife resurging with all its crystals."[21] And it is that pain which wounds the deepest and, hence, awakens and revives dead muscle and now, with heart quickened, makes speak those who had always lived in silence.

The Madwomen of the Plaza de Mayo were speaking not only from the oldest square in Buenos Aires but also from an ancestral link uniting mother and child. That is why they were speaking in an incomprehensible tongue. They were not defending the family, an institution that men created at women's expense. They were shouting a displaced language which preceded social discourse and which, through the cry itself, became social discourse. That cry was articulated in the Plaza de Mayo for all to hear.

The madness of the Madwomen of the Plaza de Mayo is situated within another referential framework. These women were speaking over the head of the state directly to the feelings and conscience of the nation. The state employed no logic to condemn the madwomen; it simply ignored them, just as it ignored the unchangeable reality of a dead child. The madness that earned them the title of madwomen is their allegiance to another sense of reality, one that now earned them another title, that of "the Mothers of the Plaza de Mayo."

The mothers of the Plaza de Mayo had nothing to do with feminism, although their actions were contemporary with it. The Argentina of the 1970s was engulfed in mourning, and not in the happiness mixed with anguish with which women in wealthy countries were discovering the possibility of new horizons. Except for those engaged in the battle for human rights, women in northern countries were largely unaware of the importance for them of what was going on in a plaza in South America.

In 1980, the United Nations convened a women's conference on peace in Vienna. There seemed to be a consensus from the outset that women's presence would be important to the establishment of peace, although there hovered over those of us who were delegates the uncomfortable ghost of a memory: the acts of violence being committed by women in power, such as Indira Gandhi and Margaret Thatcher. Nevertheless, the very idea of the conference reinforced the feeling that the presence of women in the decision-making process would be sufficient to resist the notion of war.

All this seemed both right and wrong to me, and yet I didn't know why. I recall that I paid an emotional tribute on the floor to the Madwomen of the Plaza de Mayo, a tribute to the women of my continent. When I returned to my seat, a North American delegate seated beside me asked who these women were. When she went to the podium next, she presented endless statistics on the number of women occupying positions in the legislative and executive branches, from the federal level down to the most isolated county of Idaho; then she underlined the salary inequities and the difficulties women faced as they tried to move up in the system. At the end of the afternoon, as I contemplated the opposite bank of the Danube, I began to ponder the distance separating our discourses and how foreign they were to each other. The North American feminist knew nothing about the Madwomen of the Plaza de Mayo; likewise, her statistics left me cold, bored, with a feeling of "more of the same."

Of course I empathized with the efforts of North American women to struggle against widespread, political ostracism and their desire to become a part, or how they thought they were becoming a part, of the decision-making process. Of course I supported, and would continue to support, all the demands to move in this direction. However, I couldn't help but ask myself how it was possible that a North American delegate, one who was already part of the decision-making process, could be unaware of what seemed to me to be the apparent emergence of the feminine in the political arena. Nor did her quantitative view of the achievements of feminism give me any consolation. At that moment I realized that feminism would only make an impact if it brought to politics not a new squadron of politicians in skirts but some more fundamental issues. What was needed was the recognition of a logic removed from politics and closer to ethics, perhaps the only logic capable of revitalizing politics. It occurred to me then that as women expressed themselves more freely on such unusual issues, the more thoroughly the idea of democracy would be interrogated.

Democracy could no longer be guaranteed by the simple quantitative presence of women in the public sphere. That presence is nothing more than a starting point, an early demand, the prehistory of democracy. It is clear that without the physical presence of women in the representative and executive ranks of society, we would return to the age of sexual apartheid against which feminists have been struggling for more than a century; and before that, so many women struggled that they were all given the epithet of madwomen.

The defense of equal opportunity was once intended to correct historical errors and promote equality. Likewise, the quota system, which today represents a far-reaching vindication of the politics of equality, is a kind of maximum realization of the quantitative indicator of equality. The quota system can be credited with having opened up the space within which a fluke might occur. That fluke would consist of an about-face in the ways women have been behaving in the political arena. Perhaps this about-face will be possible when women come to power imbued not only with the spirit of equality but with the desire to exercise difference. Quantitative equality has been impacting the process of women's political participation; the politics of difference needs to consider the content of this process.

It is important to recognize that, until now, much of women's energy on their political journey went into insuring that very journey, into guaranteeing that women could be elected deputy or governor, or even prime minister. Just as in a simple mathematical equation, it was believed that when a majority of women acquired decision-making power, the interests of women in general would automatically be represented. That was not, is not, and will never be true as long as we require of our female politicians merely that they belong to a certain gender and have the right to escape the limits of that gender to act like men.

The interests of women will be represented when a woman in a position of power is capable of acting like a woman by challenging all the cultural stereotypes that reduce feminine logic to the irrational and that regard feminine sensibility as excessive sentimentality; when women in power make feminine culture exist in open negotiation with masculine culture. We will be able to speak of democracy only when different views of the world and societal organization come together to seek common solutions. The feminine in politics thus takes the form of a vindication of democracy that will lead us out of a neolithic age of democracy and allow us to envision a certain modernity. Because for women it is not a question of entering politics like well-behaved students trying to speak masculine without an accent—*peau noire, masque blanc*. It is not a question of becoming involved in the political machinery but rather, perhaps, stalling it out so that an alternate machine, one which women can operate, becomes essential.

Antigone was the work of a man, as was the disheveled mother in Picasso's *Guernica*. Úrsula Iguarán, invading the barracks and whipping her tyrannical great-grandson in the yard, gave birth to García Márquez. These were artistic sublimations of a premonition of the feminine that lived, like unforgettable, archetypal creatures as tenants in the bodies of those men.

The political fact created by the Madwomen of the Plaza de Mayo is the work of women. Art made life, the feminine made politics. It was dawn in the Plaza de Mayo of Buenos Aires when a group of women slipped toward the front of the palace and into history.

Antigone and the Androgyne

CHAPTER 5

True equality between men and women implies neither androgyny nor the elimination of differences. The attempt to lay the foundation for relations between the sexes through elimination of gender differences fortunately breaks down into alterity based on the irreducible reality of the body.

In recovering the myth of the androgyne, Suzanne Lilar recalls that for many cultures the inception of human history begins with the loss of unity represented in the figure of the androgyne, which gives way to the duality manifested in the existence of the sexes. Desire is the tragic nostalgia for that first undifferentiated wholeness, the élan for the reencounter with lost unity.

The Greeks defined reality as the contrast between opposing forces and understood that opposites attract and belong to each other. One is not, and is not becoming, the other. Just as women are becoming other women, men can become other men. This does not imply that men and women will someday blend into one another. Any attempt to dissolve and fuse men and women, the masculine and feminine, into an undifferentiated magma of human nature would break down the very dynamics of life. One of the main characteristics of the masculine cultural universe has been, precisely, its arrogant and distant attitude vis-à-vis nature. Masculine culture never sought an understanding nor an equilibrium with nature because, in its arrogance, it didn't feel itself a part of nature. Contemporary ecological movements have done nothing but condemn that misunderstanding, that pretext by which our civilization placed itself in opposition to nature. In this way, ecologists today have become the allies of women who are intent on feminizing the world.

These women may be the first to confront the highly delicate problem of nature since, for women, nature has always been a taboo subject. The appraisal of female nature has always been the favorite argument of the most reactionary thought. It served to immobilize history, to refer to an immutable essence, to glorify the eternal feminine. It served primarily to forbid women any movement beyond the space that nature supposedly had reserved for them. Feminism, in the tradition of progressive thought, systematically opposed any attempt to assess female nature. It waged combat without quarter against the defenders of conservative thought. Feminism opposed any interpretation of nature that would transform the female body into a prison and legitimize inequality in the social and political status between men and women.

The enshrinement of maternity was accompanied by a whole ideology of submission, conformity, and acceptance of borders. Today, I take up once again the theme of nature, but this time from a different perspective. I refer not to a limiting, adversarial nature but to a partner, a companion nature. It's a question of destroying the arrogant paradigm by which human beings excluded themselves from nature, positioned themselves outside of it, whether to deny it or to defy it. It's a matter of breaking down the opposition of nature and culture, to find ourselves pleasantly surprised in the middle of a human history of nature in which nature is neither ignored nor eliminated but respected by the human choices made throughout history. A human history of nature includes the history of the feminine, the feminine as history.

Today, the feminine is no longer the other nor the same as the masculine. Rather than an essence linked to an immutable nature, the feminine is an experience linked to a historical nature. In this fashion, the feminine enters into a free space where it is more correct to speak of what is not conceptualized than the absence of a concept. The feminine will be free in the future to define itself in reference to nature as an experience, not as an essence. The feminine will not deny the primordial place of the body through which it lives and reflects upon the world, but will integrate it into its outlook on the world. The feminine will not deny the past, the feminine culture that subsisted on the periphery of the world of men, but neither will it accept this culture as an alibi for exclusion and confinement. To integrate the human history of feminine nature into the design of the future of the feminine constitutes a project at once feminist and ecological. Women's greatest historical victory in the twentieth century was winning their social voice. The twenty-first century opens with a new hope: that the feminine voice will not be merely the absurd echo of an absurd world. It is expected that women will have a revolutionary sociocultural impact on the world: creativity in all areas of existence, in the relationships between people, in the multiple faces of love, in the social organization of society and in the workplace—where both men and women earn their living and lose their lives—as well as in the weighty political decisions in which the peace and survival of the planet will be decided.

Feminism would not have gotten very far had it worn itself out in a banal imitation of the world of men. The work of creativity, of reflection, the boldness to propose what is apparently unlikely, must nurture feminism in the years to come, must elaborate new platforms just as some years ago we proclaimed, "our bodies, ourselves." In the coming years, women who set out to feminize the world will probably reencounter their previously known minority status, along with the whole burden of originality and differentiation that characterizes that status: a radical desire enveloped in a utopian aura.

As they search for the feminine, women will once again take up their struggle against the androgyne, for only in the passage through the feminine is it possible to reach the androgyne. The androgyne which they are promising us today is a kind of freak generated in this century, misshapen, unlike the perfect, harmonious being that mythology has bequeathed to us. In that creature, its unflawed balance between the feminine and the masculine suggests a cyclical, integrated, fused form. The androgyne of our time has the face of a man, it conceals the feminine like a deformity, an abnormality, an error, a flaw, an absence. The mythological androgyne, balanced and equidistant from the circle, turned like a wheel on its multiple feet. The modern androgyne limps, some of its feet are longer and more solid than others, and they are the ones that determine its rhythm and its gait. Sacrificed by a decisive cut, made man and woman, the mythological androgyne wanders about disconsolate, mutilated, weeping, and seeking its lost half. And when it finds the other half it embraces it tenderly, and that is the history of love.

The modern androgyne had another destiny. Separated, its halves endured such acrimonious discord that once reunited they no longer form a perfect fit. In the modern androgyne the male half absorbs the female half, or it acts as if only one sex existed where once there existed two.

Yes, the modern androgyne is a distortion. Yet, the other

one, the mythical one, survives as a myth. The scar of the androgyne has never healed in any of us. Hence, we seek, somewhere in time, to recreate the perfect balance, celebrate the lost harmony that would permit the advent of love. But that love comes with strings attached. Androgyny would be possible only if Antigone were happy.

NOTES

Translator's Preface

1. Darcy de Oliveira has discussed her European exile in several interviews. See, for example, the interview with Maurício Dias, "Confissões feministas," *Jornal do Brasil* (December 4, 1994). I have drawn freely, but not exclusively, from this interview in order to synthesize the author's views for the English reader.
2. Miguel Darcy de Oliveira, "Crise ou transformação?" in *Transformação* (Rio de Janeiro, IDAC, 1993), 146.
3. Dias, 3
4. Dias, 5
5. I have also drawn freely on Regina Zappa's interview with Darcy de Oliveira. See "A contribuição da diferença," *Jornal do Brasil*, 18 June 1995.
6. Rosiska Darcy de Oliveira, "Women and Nature: an ancestral bond, a new alliance," in *Terra Femina*, ed. Rosiska Darcy de Oliveira and Thais Corral (Rio de Janeiro, IDAC, 1992), 81.

CHAPTER 1 **Introduction**

1. Clarice Lispector, *The Passion According to G.H.*, trans. Ronald Sousa (Minneapolis: University of Minnesota Press, 1988), 127.
2. Lispector, *The Passion According to G.H.*, v.

CHAPTER 2 **Sexual Dichotomy and Inequality**

1. Sophocles, *Antigone*, trans. Andrew Brown (Warminster, Wiltshire: Aris and Phillips, 1987), 25.
2. *Antigone*, 61.
3. *Antigone*, 77.
4. *Antigone*, 93–97.
5. George Steiner, *Antigones* (New York: Oxford University Press, 1984).
6. See Margaret Mead, *Male and Female* (New York: William Morrow &

Co., 1949), and *Sex Differences*, ed. P. Lee and R. Steward (New York: Urizen Books, 1976).
7. George Balandier, *Anthropologiques* (Paris: Presses Universitaires de France, 1974), 14.
8. Edgar Morin, *Le paradigme perdu: la nature humaine* (Paris: Seuil, 1973), 79.
9. Serge Moscovici, *Society Against Nature* (London: The Harvester Press, 1976), 71.
10. Morin, 175–176.
11. Claude Lévi-Strauss, *The Elementary Structures of Kinship* (Boston: The Beacon Press, 1969), 115–116.
12. Moscovici, *Society Against Nature*, 106–107.
13. Moscovici, *Society Against Nature*, 122–123. For the original, more extensive version, see Moscovici, *La société contre nature* (Paris: Union Générale d'Éditions, 1972), 115–116.
14. Mead, 102–103.
15. Elisabeth Badinter, *L'un est l'autre* (Paris: Jacob, 1986); [*Man/Woman: The One Is the Other*, trans. Barbara Wright (London: Collins Harvill, 1989), 109.]
16. George Lapassade, *L'entrée dans la vie* (Paris: Minuit, 1963), 87.
17. Odette Thibault, "Le fait biologique," In *Le fait féminin*, ed. Evelyne Sullerot (Paris: Fayard, 1968), 27.
18. Evelyne Sullerot, *Histoire et sociologie du travail féminin* (Paris: Gonthier, 1986), 33.
19. Virginia Woolf, *A Room of One's Own* (New York: Harcourt Brace Jovanovich, 1929), 80–81.
20. See E. Erikson, *Childhood and Society* (New York: Norton, 1950), and "Psychosocial Identity" in *International Encyclopedia of Social Sciences*, ed. D. L. Sills (Macmillan and the Free Press, 1968).
21. M. Zavalloni, "L'identité psycho-sociale, un concept à la recherche d'une science" in *Introduction à la psychologie sociale*, ed. Serge Moscovici (Paris: Larousse, 1973), 246–247.
22. Herbert Marcuse, *Actuels* (Paris: Seuil, 1975), 43.

CHAPTER 3   **The Equality Trap**
1. The Three Marias, Maria Isabel Barreno, Maria Teresa Horta, Maria Velho da Costa. *New Portuguese Letters*, trans. Helen R. Lane (London: Doubleday & Co., 1975), 317.
2. "Feminiser le monde,"*Documents* IDAC, 10 (Geneva: Institut d'Action Culturelle, 1975).
3. "Feminiser le monde."
4. "Feminiser le monde."
5. "Feminiser le monde."
6. "Feminiser le monde."
7. Serge Moscovici, *Psychologie des minorités actives* (Paris: PUF, 1979), 11. For Moscovici's discussion on this topic in English, see *Social Influence and Social Change*, trans. Carol Sherrard and Greta Heinz (London, New York, and San Francisco: Academic Press, 1976), 2.

8. See *Social Influence and Social Change*, 192.
9. See *Social Influence and Social Change*, 192–193.
10. In a lecture published in *Recontres Internationales de Genève*, 1985, Maria de Lourdes Pintasilgo first used the term "unprecedented and subversive equality" to characterize the recognition of difference without hierarchy as the touchstone of female identity.
11. J. Laplanche and J.-B. Pontalis, *The Language of Psycho-analysis*, trans. Donald Nicholson Smith (New York: W. W. Norton & Co., 1973), 28.
12. J. Bleger, *Symbiose et ambiguité* (Paris: PUF, 1981), 208.
13. Bleger, 211.
14. See Gregory Bateson, *Steps to an Ecology of Mind* (Northvale, N. J., and London: Jason Aronson, 1987), 208.
15. Bleger, 223.
16. Yvonne Verdier, *Façons de dire, façons de faire* (Paris: Gallimard: 1979).
17. Robin Lakoff, *Language and Woman's Place* (New York: Harper and Row, 1975), 3.
18. Lakoff, 4.
19. N. Henley, "Power, Sex and Nonverbal Communication," *Berkeley Journal of Sociology*, 1973–1974, 18:1–26.
20. See Marina Yaguyello, *Les mots et les femmes* (Paris: Payot, 1978), and Carol Gilligan, *In a Different Voice* (Cambridge: Harvard University Press, 1982).
21. Matina Horner, "Fail: Bright Women," *Psychology Today*, 3, 6 (Nov. 1969), and "Towards an Understanding of Achievement-Related Conflicts in Women," *Journal of Social Issues*, 28 (1972):157–175.
22. Judith Bardwick, *Women in Transition* (Brighton, U.K.: The Harvester Press, 1980), 51–52.
23. Bardwick, 52.
24. Colette Dowling, *The Cinderella Complex* (New York: Pocket Books, 1981), 172.
25. Dowling, 178.
26. For an in-depth discussion of Oliveira's views on ambiguity, see *Le féminin ambigu* (Geneva: Editions du Concept Moderne, 1989).

CHAPTER 4 **The Emergence of the Feminine**
1. Badinter, *L'un est l'autre*; trans. by Barbara Wright *Man/Woman: The One Is the Other* (London: Collins Harvill, 1989).
2. *Man/Woman*, 174.
3. Luce Irigaray, *This Sex Which Is Not One*, trans. Catherine Porter and Carolyn Burke (Ithaca, N.Y.: Cornell University Press, 1977).
4. "Faire le ménage, c'est travailler," *Cahiers du Grif*, 14 (Belgium: Groupe Recherche Information Femmes).
5. André Gorz, *Critique of Economic Reason*, trans. Gillian Handyside and Chris Turner (London: Verso, 1989). 136.
6. Gorz, 137.
7. See Gorz's discussion on economically rational work, 137–138; I have drawn freely on his vocabulary in this passage.

8. Virginia Woolf, *A Room of One's Own* (New York: Harcourt Brace, 1929).
9. Marguerite Yourcenar, *With Open Eyes*, trans. Arthur Goldhammer (Boston: Beacon Press, 1984), 10.
10. Published by Farrar, Straus, & Giroux, both novels have been translated into English by Grace Frick in collaboration with the author. See *Memoirs of Hadrian*, 1954, 1957, 1963 and *The Abyss*, 1976.
11. Patrick de Rosbo, *Entrevistas com Marguerite Yourcenar* (Rio de Janeiro: Editora Nova Fronteira, 1987). The original French publication is titled *Entretiens radiophoniques avec Marguerite Yourcenar* (Mercure de France, 1972). For Yourcenar's comments on the character of Hadrian, see *With Open Eyes*, 113–129.
12. *Entrevistas com Marguerite Yourcenar*. For Yourcenar's comments on the absence of exceptional women in history, the reader may consult "And Feminism?" in *With Open Eyes*, 221–227.
13. Marcelle Marini, *Territoires du féminin avec M. Duras* (Paris: Laffont, 1979).
14. Luce Irigaray, *Speculum of the Other Woman*, trans. Gillian C. Gill (Ithaca, N.Y.: Cornell University Press, 1985).
15. Hélène Cixous, *Coming to Writing and Other Essays*, ed. Deborah Jenson, trans. Sarah Cornell et al. (Cambridge, Mass.: Harvard University Press, 1991), 52
16. *Souffles* (Paris: Edition des femmes, 1995). See the back cover of the novel.
17. Yvonne Verdier, *Façons de faire, façons de dire* (Paris: Gallimard, 1979).
18. Rainer Maria Rilke, *Letter to a Young Poet*, trans. Stephen Mitchell (New York: Random House, 1984), 107.
19. Hélène Cixous, "The Laugh of the Medusa" in *New French Feminisms: An Anthology*, ed. Elaine Marks and Isabelle de Courtivron (Brighton, Sussex: Harvester Press, 1981), 245.
20. The Plaza de Mayo (literally, "May Square") is the large, principal city square in the older part of Buenos Aires, the capital city of Argentina. The Cabildo (or, "Town Hall") is one of the oldest buildings in the city, dating from the colonial period when it housed the town council. The Casa Rosada ("The Pink House") is the presidential palace, sort of an equivalent of the White House in the United States, although the Argentine president does not actually reside there. The color refers to the faded pinkish tone of the original colonial adobe construction used in many Latin American buildings. The cathedral also faces on the square.
21. These lines are from João Cabral de Melo Neto's famous poem "Uma faca só lamina," which has been translated by John Nist as "Only the Blade of a Knife," in *Modern Brazilian Poetry: An Anthology*, trans. and ed. John Nist (Bloomington: Indiana University Press, 1962), 145–158.

BIBLIOGRAPHY

Ardoino, J. *Education e Politique*. Paris: Gauthier-Villars, 1975.
Bachelard, G. *La psychanalyse du feu*. Paris: Gallimard, 1949.
———. *Le nouvel esprit scientifique*. Paris: P.U.F., 1966.
Badinter, E. *L'amour en plus*. Paris: Flammarion, 1980.
———. *L'un est l'autre*. Paris: Jacob, 1986. [*Man/Woman: The One is the Other*, trans. Barbara Wright. London: Collins Harvill, 1989.]
Balandier, G. *Anthropologiques*. Paris: P.U.F.: 1974.
Barbier, R. *La recherche-action dans l'institution educative*. Paris: Gauthier Villars, 1977.
Bardwick, N. *Women in Transition*. Brighton, U. K.: The Harvester Press, 1980.
Bateson, G. *Vers une écologie de l'esprit*. Paris: Seuil, 1980.
Beauvoir, S. de. *Le deuxième sexe*. Paris: Seuil, 1980.
Belotti, E.G. *Dalle parte delle bambine*. Milan: Feltrinelli, 1973.
———. *Prima le donne e i bambini*. Milan: Rizzoli, 1980.
Bernstein, B. *Class, Codes and Control*. Boston: Routledge and Kegan, 1970.
Bion, W.R. *Aux sources de l'experience*. Paris: P.U.F., 1965.
———. *Recherche sur les petits groupes*. Paris: P.U.F., 1965.
Bleger, J. *Symbiose et ambiguité*. Paris: P.U.F., 1965.
Bourdieu, P., J.-C. Chamboredon, and J.-C. Passeron. *Le métier de sociologue*. Paris: Mouton, 1968.
Brownmiller, S. *Femininity*. New York: Ballantine, 1985.
Burr E., S. Dunn, and N. Farquhar. "Women and the Language of Inequality." *Social Education* 36 (1972):841–845.
Cardinet, J., J. Weiss. "L'observation interactive, au confluent de la formation et de la recherche." *Les sciences de l'éducation* 1–2 (1979):177–203.
Cixous, H. *Souffles*. Paris: Des femmes, 1975.
Conklin, N. "Towards a Feminist Analysis of Linguistic Behavior." *The University of Michigan Papers in Women's Studies* 1, 1 (1974):51–73.

Darcy de Oliveira, R. "L'observation militante: Une alternative sociologique." *IDAC* 9 (1974).
———. "Education et sociétés." *Le bureau international de l'éducation au service du mouvement éducatif.* UNESCO, 1979.
———. "Les femmes en mouvement et l'avenir de l'éducation." *Cahiers de la Section des Sciences de l'Education* 14. Geneva: University of Geneva, 1979.
———. "Pesquisa social e ação educativa." *Pesquisa Participante.* São Paulo: Brasiliense, 1980.
———. *Mulher, sexo no feminino.* São Paulo: Brasiliense, 1981.
———. "Les pierres dans la poche du féminisme." *Cahiers de la Section des Sciences de l'Education* 38. Geneva: University of Geneva, 1985.
Dominice, P. *La formation enjeu de l'évaluation.* Berne-Frankfurt/Main: Peter Lang, 1979.
———. "Quelques remarques sur la recherche-action." *Cahiers de la Section des Sciences de l'Education* 26. Geneva: University of Geneva, 1981.
Dowling. C. *Le complexe de Cendrillon.* Paris: Seuil, 1982.
Durkheim, E. *Les règles de la méthode sociologique.* Paris: P.U.F., 1963.
———. *Education et sociologie.* Paris: P.U.F., 1977.
d'Eaubonne, F. *Les femmes avant le patriarchat.* Paris: Payot, 1976.
Engels, F. *Les origines de la famille, de la propriéte privée et de l'état.* Paris: Editions Sociales, 1954.
Erikson, E. *Childhood and Society.* New York: W. W. Norton, 1963.
———. *Identity and the Life Cycle.* New York: W. W. Norton, 1968.
———. *Identity, Youth and Crisis.* New York: W. W. Norton, 1968.
Fals Borda, O. *Causa Popular, Ciencia Popular.* Bogotá: Rosca, 1972.
"Féminiser le monde." *IDAC* (1976).
Finkielkraut, A. *La défaite de la pensée.* Paris: Gallimard, 1987.
Firestone, S. *The Dialectic of Sex.* New York: Morrow, 1970.
Foucault, M. *Histoire de la sexualité: La volonté de savoir,* vol. 1. Paris: Gallimard, 1976.
Freire, P. *L'éducation pratique de la liberté.* Paris: Cerf, 1971.
———. *Pédagogie des opprimés.* Paris: Maspero, 1974.
———. *Ação cultural para a libertação.* Rio de Janeiro: Paz e Terra, 1977.
Freud, S. *Trois essais sur la théorie de la sexualité.* Paris: Gallimard, 1962.
———. *Nouvelles conférences sur la psychanalyse.* Paris: Gallimard, 1962.
———. *La vie sexuelle.* Paris: P.U.F., 1969.
Friedan, B. *The Feminine Mystique.* New York: Norton, 1963.
Galli, G.A. *Come si fa ricerca.* Milan: Mondadori, 1979.
Gilligan, C. *Une si grande différence.* Paris: Flammarion, 1986.
Habermas, J. *Kultur und Kritik.* Frankfurt am Main: Suhrkamp, 1973.
———. *La technique et la science comme idéologie.* Paris: Gallimard, 1973.
———. *L'espace public.* Paris: Payot, 1978.
———. *Theory of Communicative Action.* London: Heinemann, 1984.
Halimi, G. *La cause des femmes.* Paris: Grasset, 1973.

Hall, B. "Participatory Research: An Approach for Change." *Convergence* 2 (1975).
Hays, H.R. *The Dangerous Sex: The Myth of Feminine Evil*. New York: Putnam, 1964.
Henley, N. "Power, Sex and Nonverbal Communication." *Berkeley Journal of Sociology* 18 (1973/74):1–26.
———. "The Sexual Politics of Interpersonal Behavior." In J. Freeman, ed., *Women: A Feminist Perspective*. Palo Alto: Mayfield, 1975.
Horkheimer, M. *Théorie traditionnelle et théorie critique*. Paris: Gallimard, 1974.
Illich, I. *Une société sans école*. Paris: Seuil, 1971.
———. *Gender*. London: Boyars, 1982.
Jacob, F. *La logique du vivant*. Paris: Gallimard, 1970.
Janeway, F. *Man's World, Woman's Place*. New York: Dell, 1971.
Key, M.R. "Linguistic Behavior of Male and Female." *Linguistics* 88 (1972):15–31.
Klein, M. *Envy and Gratitude*. London: Tavistock, 1957.
Labov, W. *Sociolinguistic Patterns*. Philadelphia: University of Pennsylvania Press, 1972.
Lakoff, R. *Language and Woman's Place*. New York: Harper and Row, 1975.
Lapassade, G. *L'entrée dans la vie*. Paris: Minuit, 1963.
Leclerc, A. *Parole de femme*. Paris: Grasset, 1974.
———. *Hommes et femmes*. Paris: Grasset, 1985.
Lee, P. and R. Steward, eds. *Sex Differences*. New York: Urizen Books, 1976.
Lévi-Strauss, C. *Anthropologie structurale*. Paris: Plon, 1958.
———. *La pensée sauvage*. Paris: Plon, 1962.
———. *Les structures élémentaires de la parenté*. Paris: Mouton, 1967.
Malinowski, B. *Sex, Culture, and Myth*. New York: Harcourt Brace, 1962.
Marcuse, H. *Eros and Civilization*. Boston: Beacon Press, 1974.
———. *Actuels*. Paris: Seuil, 1975.
Marini, M. *Territoires du féminin*. Paris: Minuit, 1977.
Mead, M. *Male and Female*. New York, Morrow, 1949.
Mendel, G. *Quand plus rien ne va de soi*. Paris: Laffont, 1979.
Michel, A. *Les femmes dans la société marchande*. Paris: P.U.F., 1978.
———. *Sociologie de la famille et du mariage*. Paris: P.U.F., 1972.
———. *Le féminisme*. Paris: P.U.F., 1979.
Mitchell, J. *Woman's Estate*. London: Penguin, 1971.
Millett, K. *Sexual Politics*. Garden City, N.Y.: Doubleday, 1971.
Monod, J. *Le hasard et la nécessité*. Paris: Seuil, 1973.
Morin, E. *Le paradigme perdu: la nature humaine*. Paris: Seuil, 1970.
———. *L'esprit du temps*. Paris: Grasset, 1975.
———. *La méthode: la nature de la nature,* 1. Paris: Seuil, 1977.
———. *La méthode: la vie de la vie,* 2. Paris Seuil, 1980.
———. *La méthode: la connaissance de la conaissance,* 3. Paris: Seuil, 1986.
Moscovici, S. *Histoire humaine de la nature*. Paris: Flammarion, 1968.
———. *La société contre nature*. Paris: UGE, 1972. [*Society Against Nature*. London: The Harvester Press, 1976.]

———, ed. *Introduction à la psychologie sociale*. Paris: Larousse, 1973.
———. *Hommes domestiques, hommes sauvages*. Paris: UGE, 1974.
———. "Le réenchantemente du monde." *Au-delà de la crise*. Paris: Seuil, 1975.
———. *Psychologie des minorités actives*. Paris: P.U.F., 1979.
Murstein, B. *Styles de vie intime*. Brussels: Mardaga, 1981.
Piaget, J. *Epistémologie des sciences de l'homme*. Paris: Gallimard, 1970.
Pineau, G. *Vies des histoires de vie*. Université de Montréal. Faculté d'Education Permanente, 1980.
Prieto, L. *Pertinence et pratique*. Paris: Minuit, 1975.
"Promotion socio-culturelle des femmes en formation." C.C.C., Conseil de l'Europe, 1981.
"Recherche-Action: interrogations et stratégies émergeantes." *Cahiers de la Section des Sciences de l'Education 26*. Geneva: University of Geneva, 1981.
Reed, E. *Problems of Women's Liberation*. New York: Pathfinder Press, 1971.
Reed, E. *Feminisme et anthropologie*. Paris: Denoël-Gonthier, 1979.
Reik, T. "Men and Women Speak Different Languages." *Psychoanalysis* 2, 4 (1954):3–15.
Reik, T. *Myth and Guilt*. New York, Braziller, 1960.
Reik T. *The Temptation*. New York: Braziller 1961.
Revue Internationale d'Action Communitaire: La recherche-action, enjeux et perspectives. Special Number 5/45 (spring 1981).
Rich, A. *Of Woman Born*. New York: Norton, 1976.
———. *On Lies, Secrets, Silence*. New York: W. W. Norton, 1979.
Rogers, C. *Les groupes de Renomine*. Paris: Dunod, 1980.
Rowbotham, S. *Women, Resistance and Revolution*. Vintage Books, 1974.
Saussure, F. *Cours de linguistique générale*. Paris: Payot, 1962.
Stavenhagen, R. "Comment décoloniser les sciences sociales." *Sept thèses erronées sur l'Amérique Latine*. Paris: Anthropos, 1972.
Sullerot, E. *Demain les femmes*. Paris: Laffont, 1965.
———. *Histoire et sociologie du travail féminin*. Paris: Gonthier, 1968.
———, ed. *Le fait féminin*. Paris: Fayard, 1978.
———. *Pour le meilleur et sans le pire*. Paris: Fayard, 1984.
Thibault, O. *L'homme inachevé*. Paris: Casterman, 1972.
———. *Debout les femmes*. Lyon: Chronique Sociales, 1980.
Thorn, B. and N. Henley, Ed. *Language and Sex: Difference and Dominance*. Rowley, Mass: Newbury House, 1975.
Touraine, A. *La voix et le regard*. Paris: Seuil, 1978.
Troutot, P.Y. "Sociologie d'intervention et recherche-action socio-politique." *Revue Suisse de Sociologie* (1980).
Verdier, Y. *Façons de dire, façons de faire*. Paris: Gallimard, 1979.
Vetterlin-Braggin, M., ed. *Sexist Language*. Adams, 1981.
Woolf, V. *A Room of One's Own*. New York: Harcourt Brace, 1929.
Yaguello, M. *Les mots et les femmes*. Paris: Payot, 1978.

ABOUT THE AUTHOR

Rosiska Darcy de Oliveira is a lawyer, activist, writer, international consultant, and a professor of literature at the *Pontífica Universidade Católica* of Rio de Janeiro. With Paulo Freire, she cofounded IDAC (Institute for Cultural Action) during her exile in Europe. Darcy de Oliveira is the leading spokesperson for women's rights and the environmental protection movement in Brazil. In 1995, she was named President of the National Council on Women's Rights, a federally sponsored initiative headquartered at the Ministry of Justice in Brasília.

About the Translator

Peggy Sharpe is an associate professor of Portuguese and Women's Studies at the University of Illinois at Urbana-Champaign where she teaches the literature, film, culture, and language of the Portuguese-speaking world. Her research examines the writings and transformation of cultural practices among Brazilian women in the nineteenth and twentieth centuries.